Cultivating a Good Family Heritage

Leaving your Children a Legacy to Cherish

Armand and Kathy Tiffe

Cultivating a Good Family Heritage

Leaving your Children a Legacy to Cherish

Cover Design by Kymm Tingum

ISBN: 978-1-936141-59-3

PRINTED IN THE UNITED STATES OF AMERICA
By
FOCUS PUBLISHING
Bemidji, Minnesota

To Gabriel, Natalie, Oliver, Joel, and Stefan

"Grandchildren are the crown of the aged."

Proverbs 17:6

Endorsements

Here is a wealth of practical, common sense counsel for parents which, most important of all, is built upon the riches of biblical wisdom. In this little book, the authors share their decades of personal experience as parents, grandparents, and biblical counselors with other Christian parents who want to leave their children something infinitely more important than a material inheritance. *Cultivating a Good Family Heritage* is a large gift of encouragement and instruction wrapped in a small package.

> **Paul Tautges,** Author; Senior Pastor, Cornerstone Community Church, Mayfield Heights, Ohio; Founder, *Counseling One Another*

What a great idea for a book in our perilous times! Armand and Kathy not only have a great idea for a book, but they have delivered an excellent resource with biblical wisdom and practical ways to grow a family God's way, and for His glory. Any modern family will benefit from putting into practice the simple, clear examples of cultivating a family. It is not difficult to do, but requires a change in philosophy and priority that is based in sound theology. It is never too late for any family to implement the strategies discovered in this indispensable resource.

> **Mark E. Shaw, D. Min.** , Founder of The Addiction Connection (www.theaddictionconnection.org), Director of Counseling at Grace Fellowship Church in Florence, KY, and author of 23 publications including *Addiction-Proof Parenting* and *The Heart of Addiction*

Armand and Kathy Tiffe have written a Scripture saturated book on the family. This book resonated with me on so many levels! It is the resource I wished for when I was raising a family. I highly endorse this book, and plan to make it required reading for the students in our parenting module.

> **Dr. Julie Ganschow**, Author, *The Process of Biblical Change* and *Seeing Depression Through the Eyes of Grace*

This book is short, but it packs a punch. Page after page has encouraged us and spurred us on as parents of two young children. It's full of practical ideas on how to have a happy, God-honoring home. Put down your phones and grab this book. You won't regret it, and it will leave you wanting more!

> **Sean and Jennifer Perron**, Pastor and wife counselors with the Association of Certified Biblical Counselors. Sean is the co-author of three books in the *Letters to a Romantic* series.

Armand and Kathy Tiffe have put together a marvelous book on parenting that is markedly different from many in the current Christian marketplace. They give the "big picture" of the kind of legacy God wants parents to pass on to their children, and the "details" with many suggestions and ideas to help parents work toward that goal and love the process! This book is worth adding to your must-read pile.

> **Joe Propri,** Founding Director of the Biblical Counseling Institute of Northeast Ohio; author of *The Peace and Joy Principle: How to Be Content in Any Situation*

Table of Contents

Introduction

The year was 1983. We were blissfully married for about 18 months when the phone rang in the early hours of the morning that woke us out of a sound sleep. Kathy's younger sister, Mary, was on the other end and spoke words that rocked our world — "Mom stopped breathing." At the young age of 50, Kathy's mother died of melanoma. Seven months later, her 51-year-old father would also die of pancreatic cancer. It was a life-altering year.

Following that difficult year, I (Kathy) was sifting through family photos, and I began to reflect upon family memories and the kind of heritage that was passed on to me. I thought of the good and the bad, the positive and negative. And even though Armand and I did not have children of our own at that time, we began to talk about the kind of heritage we would want to pass on should God bless us with children.

Well, He did! A year later, our first child, Anna, was born, and 15 months following our son, Armand, was born. It was a joyful time! And, once again, those thoughts of cultivating a good family heritage for our children began to resurface. As a young dad and mom, we found ourselves in a position of wanting to give our children a rich legacy consisting of close family ties, cherished memories, and biblical values.

That was our desire and something we discussed often, but struggled with questions such as, "Where would we begin? Is it possible even if we did not have the 'perfect home life' model to follow?" And, most importantly, "What would this look like in day-to-day living?"

Cultivating a Good Family Heritage is our attempt to answer these questions by giving practical ideas for everyday family life. It is our prayer that this book will be helpful to parents from any background or upbringing, and encourage parents that cultivating a good family heritage is attainable.

CHAPTER 1

Defining the Elements of a Good Family Heritage

Let's begin by clarifying the sense in which we are using the word "heritage," since there are several ways it can be understood. *Heritage* can refer to a family's genealogy, or to something of material value that is inherited from a previous generation such as property and money. However, this is *not* the sense in which we are using the word. We are referring to what we experience in our family of origin—our growing-up-years: family background, environment, character traits, family interactions, memories, and values that are passed on from parents to children.

No matter who you are or where you lived in your growing-up-years, a heritage has been passed on to you from your parents—good, bad, or some of both. And, in fact, you will pass on a heritage to your children—good, bad, or some of both—intentionally or unintentionally. As parents, we must realize that the things we do in the growing-up-years of our children will affect the way they remember their childhood. It will mold (to a large degree) who they are, how they relate to others, how they view life, and what they value. Kent and Barbara Hughes illustrate it this way:

> Psalm 127:4 compares children to arrows. Parents, like archers, launch their children into the future, aiming toward a distant target. Some parents take clear aim, and their arrows are well directed toward their future mark. But other "child arrows" are fired from undisciplined bows by parents who are, at best, ambivalent about where they came from and unsure of their aim. Their arrows waver and falter, then finally succumb to gravity with no mark in sight. They tragically prove the adage, "If you aim at nothing, you'll surely hit it."[1]

Unfortunately, many parents are not very aware of the kind of legacy they are leaving their children. Some are so absorbed with advancing their careers that they do not consider the deficiency of the heritage they are passing down until it is too late. Others may want to leave a good heritage, but need some help and direction because they did not have a good family heritage of their own. Perhaps one of your parents was abusive, had a drinking problem, or was not very involved in providing the nurture you needed. If such is the case, it can leave you wondering, "How do I pass on something I did not receive?" However, hope is not lost. God can redeem your past, and by His grace, you can begin to chart a new course.

1. Charting a New Course

That was our desire as young parents—to chart a new course. Neither of us were raised in Bible-believing Christian homes. We came from family backgrounds that were far from perfect. We came to faith in Christ as young adults, and when we had our first child, we knew we had a lot to learn. We desired to leave a rich legacy consisting of close family ties, cherished memories, and biblical values. By the grace of God, we tried to chart a new course for our family, and God has honored that.

That said, we do not want to give the impression that we were perfect parents with model children at every stage of the childrearing years. There were bumps on the road along the way. But we thank God that our adult children and their spouses are committed to Christ and growing in their faith and desire to pass on a heritage that their children will cherish.

In this book, we want to share some concrete, practical things parents can do to cultivate a good, solid family heritage. It will especially be pertinent for parents of pre-school children through early-teen-years. We will be stressing the involvement of both mom and dad because that is the ideal situation. However, we realize that there are single parents who desire to leave an enduring legacy as well. If that is your present situation, please know that many of the ideas and biblical principles in this booklet can still be applied in a single-family home. There is always hope that God helps the parent who is dependent upon Him and seeks to apply His Word. Furthermore, it will be important for parents to keep in mind that passing on a good family heritage is a long process, not an event. It will require time and consistency, but the rewards will be worth it!

Scriptures that speak to this include:

- Proverbs 1:8-9: "*Hear my son your father's instruction, and forsake not your mother's teaching, for they are a graceful garland for your head and pendants for your neck.*" Here is an example of a mother and father being deliberate in passing on a legacy of wisdom needed for life that will be a treasure and a lasting blessing to their children.

- Proverbs 17:6: "*Grandchildren are the crown of the aged, and the glory of children is their fathers.*" This describes a precious bond spanning over three generations. We sense the joy and blessing of a godly heritage passed on to each succeeding generation.

- Proverbs 24:3-4: "*By wisdom a house is built, and by understanding it is established; by knowledge the rooms are filled with all precious and pleasant riches.*" This, of course, is referring to more than the construction of a house, but building a home—a family. Just like we would follow sound principles of construction when building a house, so building a strong family that enjoys the precious and pleasant riches of relationships takes wisdom, understanding, and knowledge.

2. Three Essential Elements for Cultivating a Good Family Heritage.

A good, solid family heritage includes three essential elements: *a spirit of belonging and connectedness* in family relationships, *cherished family memories and traditions* carried into adulthood, and *instilling biblical truths and values into the lives of our children.* This, in fact, is what we see our heavenly Father model for us in

His relationship with the Old Testament nation of Israel and His relationship with the New Testament Church. One of the ways God has chosen to identify Himself most frequently is as our heavenly Father. This makes Him the ultimate role model for us as parents.

A spirit of belonging and connectedness

The Old Testament often uses familial terms to describe God's relationship with the people of Israel. They are said to be His sons or children (Exodus 4:22; Deuteronomy 14:1; Proverbs 3:12). God gave the Old Testament Jews a spirit of belonging and connectedness by singling them out as His covenant people. The heart of that relationship is found in the phrase, "*I will be your God and you shall be my people*" (Genesis 17:7-8;Leviticus 26:12; Deuteronomy 4:20; Jeremiah 11:4; Ezekiel 11:20). Not only did this covenant become the basis of the special relationship Israel would have with God, but it was also meant to give the Israelites a special bond among themselves.

The New Testament also uses familial terms to describe the church. Believers are said to be "*members of God's household*" (Ephesians 2:19) and, therefore, stand in a special relationship to Him as well as to one another. This glorious truth is stated in Romans 8:15-17:

> *You have received the Spirit of adoption as sons, by whom we cry, "Abba! Father!" The Spirit himself bears witness with our spirit that we are children of God, and if children, then heirs—heirs of God and fellow heirs with Christ* (see also, Galatians 3:29; 4:6).

Our heavenly Father has given us a new identity as His adopted sons and daughters, which results in a spirit of belonging and connectedness. We are children of the same Father. We call each other brothers and sisters. We care for one another as family, sharing goods and resources where the need arises. We enjoy and experience a special kinship by virtue of our common faith in the atoning work of Christ on the cross. The church is a community, a fellowship of people who belong to one another because they belong to God (cf. Acts 4:32; 1 Peter 2:9).

Since God the Father has modeled this for us as parents, we also need to nurture a spirit of belonging and connectedness in our family relationships.

Cherished memories and traditions

God gave memorials to Israel and the Church. These memorials are meant to aid a person's memory in preserving what is most cherished.

The element of cherished memories and traditions can be seen in the annual Jewish festivals. They were meant to celebrate and remember God's provision and great acts of deliverance on their behalf (Leviticus 23). The Passover, for example, served as a reminder of God's deliverance from their bondage in Egypt: *"This day shall be for you a memorial day, and you shall keep it as a feast to the Lord"* (Exodus 12:12-14; 13:8-10). Another example is when Israel passed over the Jordan River into the Promised Land for the first time. God commanded 12 stones to be taken from the Jordan River and piled up to serve as a memorial of His provision of safe passage across the Jordan:

> *When your children ask their fathers in times to come, "What do these stones mean," then you shall let your children know, 'Israel passed over this Jordan on dry ground.' For the Lord God dried up the waters of the Jordan for you until you passed over."*
>
> *Joshua 4:1-7, 19-24*

These memorials and traditional annual feasts were meant to give Israel a sense of solidarity and unity.

For the church, the Lord's Supper serves as a reminder (a memorial) of Christ's sacrificial death and future coming:

> *The Lord Jesus on the night when he was betrayed took bread, and when he had given thanks, he broke it, and said, "This is my body, which is for you. Do this in remembrance of me." In the same way also he took the cup, after supper, saying, "This cup is the new covenant in my blood. Do this, as often as you drink it, in remembrance of me." For as often as you eat this bread and drink the cup, you proclaim the Lord's death until he comes.*
>
> *1 Corinthians 11:23-26,* (cf. Matthew 26:26-29; Mark 14:22-25)

Providentially, God has also given us holy days (Christmas, Good Friday, and Easter) to remember and celebrate the birth, death, and resurrection of our Lord and Savior Jesus Christ. Furthermore, we experience precious memories as we develop relationships with fellow believers. We share mutual experiences as we pray together, worship together, serve together, mourn together, and celebrate together in God's family, the church.

All of this is meant to give us a sense of solidarity and unity as Christians.

Since God the Father has modeled this for us as parents, we also need to implement memories and traditions that give a sense of solidarity and unity that our children will cherish and look back on with fondness.

Biblical truths and values

God has given us timeless truths and values to embrace in Holy Scripture. Biblical truths and values shape our character and effect our conduct and behavior. They are the foundation of our moral standards. They guide us on how to live life and make choices that please and honor God. As a result, our lives will be blessed (Psalm 1:1-3; 119:1-2; James 1:21-25).

After God miraculously delivered Israel from Egyptian bondage, He charged them to be faithful to Him and to the covenant of the law He established with them. The law that God established with Israel reflected God's holy nature and values. One of the reasons God revealed His law to the Israelites was so they would be set-apart (holy, sanctified, distinguished) from other pagan nations. God's desire for the people of Israel can be summed up with the words found in Deuteronomy 10:12-13:

> *And now, Israel, what does the Lord your God require of you, but to fear the Lord your God, to walk in all his ways, to love him, to serve the Lord your God with all your heart and with all your soul, and to keep the commandments and statutes of the Lord, which I am commanding you today for your good?*

Notice, all of God's commandments and statutes for Israel were designed for their good. When Israel was faithful to God and His law, they were blessed. In contrast, when they were unfaithful, they suffered the consequences. Additionally, God established that the family was His primary way for passing on the truth of His Word from one generation to the next (Deuteronomy 6:1-9; Psalm 78:5-8).

Christians rely on the Scriptures (both Old Testament and New Testament) to grow in the knowledge of God and His will. By living "*according to your word*" we keep our way pure (Psalm 119:9). The Scriptures are "*able to make you wise for salvation through faith in Christ Jesus*" (2 Timothy 3:15). The Scriptures are God's primary means "*for teaching, for reproof, for correction, and for training in righteousness, that the man of God may be complete, equipped for every good work*" (2 Timothy 3:16-17). Those who are "*doers of the word and not hearers only...will be blessed"* (James 1:22-25). All that is necessary for eternal salvation in Christ and Christian living is set forth in Scripture. God exhorts Christian parents to pass on the essential truths of His Word to their children (Ephesians 6:1-4).

God has chosen to reveal Himself and His eternal plan in the Bible. Therefore, since God has given us the Holy Scriptures, we must then as parents be diligent in imparting its truths and values into the lives of our children, starting at the earliest possible age (cf. Deuteronomy 6:6-7; Ephesians 6:1-4; 2 Timothy 3:15). There is a no more important thing you as a parent can do for your children than to teach them biblical truths and values.

3. Following our Heavenly Father's model

Following the model our heavenly Father has provided for us, let's consider how we can apply these three essential elements to our family life. Our goal is to share some practical ways of implementing them. As a longtime pastor and pastor's wife, we have had the opportunity through the years to be involved in providing biblical counsel for many marriages and families. Much of the advice and ideas that we offer in this book are what we have found as common failures or shortsightedness in husbands and wives, and fathers and mothers. While it is not meant to be exhaustive, our prayer is that it will motivate you and give some direction in becoming *more intentional and purposeful in cultivating a good family heritage for your children*. In fact, you may find that it will stimulate some thoughts of your own.

Furthermore, as you read through this book, evaluate your areas of strengths and weaknesses. Make a conscious effort to work on the weak areas. At the end of this booklet is a supplementary list of recommended resources for further study and additional help in this great undertaking.

Essential Element 1

Cultivate a Spirit of Belonging and Connectedness in Family Relationships

In an orphanage in Bulgaria, a little girl by the name of Natalia lived the first five years of her life in a crib. She was unwanted, abandoned, neglected, and malnourished. She was an orphan. It was apparent that Natalia's repetitious hand motions, staring into space, and sensory cravings were signals that she longed for a connection with something or someone.

At the age of five, Natalia was chosen for adoption by a young couple from the United States. Part of the adoption process was that Natalia would be given a new birth certificate providing her with a new name, Natalie. She was no longer an unwanted orphan. She now belonged to a family. From that day forward, her new parents, Mike and Anna (our son-in-law and daughter), began the journey of helping our new granddaughter understand the special bond of family relationships.

Similarly, we are all like orphans, born with a sense of wanting to belong. Ultimately, God is there to meet that void by offering us salvation through His Son, Jesus Christ, and adopting us into His family. This is what God has done for those of us who have come to saving faith in Christ. Believers belong to the family of God. God is our Father. We live with the awareness of the Fatherhood of God. Therefore, we have a God-given sense of family.

> *So then you are no longer strangers and aliens, but you are fellow citizens with the saints and members of the household of God.*
>
> *Ephesians 2:19*

> *For all who are led by the Spirit of God are sons of God. For you did not receive the spirit of slavery to fall back into fear, but you have received the Spirit of adoption as sons, by whom we cry, "Abba! Father!" The Spirit himself bears witness with our spirit that we are children of God, and if children, then heirs—heirs of God and fellow heirs with Christ.*
>
> *Romans 8:14-17a*

This familial language is meant to instill within us a spirit of belonging and connectedness as beloved members of the household of God! Likewise, God graciously gives us human family relationships. This is to be viewed as a great blessing, an opportunity for parents to cultivate a spirit of belonging and connectedness in family relationships.

In this section, we will consider three ways parents can accomplish this:

- Foster a sense of family identity
- Demonstrate an ongoing love as husband and wife
- Nurture the relationship with your children

CHAPTER 2
Foster a Sense of Family Identity

A good heritage begins by establishing the identity of each member of the family as an essential part of the family. This means that we must nurture an environment where each member of the family feels like they are a part of a "team." One way you can do this is by nurturing a mindset that leads to a strong sense of family identity. Give your children the impression that God put your family together. Therefore, like team-mates, we are committed and devoted to each other. It is generally believed that negative peer pressure is minimized when a solid family identity is established. If there is not a close team-like connection in family relationships, your children will most likely find it somewhere else. It may be a group of peers that have a negative influence on them. However, when a solid family identity is established, negative peer pressure is minimized. And dads play a primary role in this.

1. Children need to observe Dad as an active member of the "Team".

Young children tend to look up to their fathers. As Proverbs 17:6 states, "*The glory of children is their fathers.*" We could paraphrase this Proverb to say, "Children take great pride in their father." What a commentary on the potential legacy of a father! His children revere him. Therefore, dads, you can have a significant impact on the lives of your children. Children need to see you as an active part of the family. They need to know that you are on the team. In fact, they need to see that you are leading the team!

The Bible teaches that fathers are to be the spiritual leaders in the home (Ephesians 5:23; 6:4; 1 Timothy 3:4). Unfortunately, too many dads are like spectators, watching mom from the sidelines as she tries to hold the family together. However, if Dad is uninvolved in the life of the family, the children will wonder if he cares, or if the family is really that important. But if Dad is excited about the family and involved in family life, the children will tend to feel the same way. If Dad is on the team, the children will be more inclined to want to be a part of the team.

One simple thing you can do as a dad is to verbalize how happy you are to be a part of such a great family. At appropriate times—when you are all gathered together as a family—you can foster a sense of family identity in your children by saying something like this: "This is such a great family. We do so many fun things together." This gives young children a sense of wanting to be a part of such a great family. Additionally, at times you can say to your children, "I'm so glad you are a part of this family. You have such a great mom. I'm so thankful that the Lord put us together as a family." In other words, talk up your family! When young children hear Dad verbalize such things, it fosters a sense of family identity. They will be happy to identify with such a terrific family, and it gives children a sense of security and confidence in knowing that dad is on the team.

2. Children need to observe Mom's joy to be on the "Team".

It is probably less often that mom's commitment to the family is in question. However, some moms tend to lose sight of the blessing and joy in raising children because of the time and energy it takes. Motherhood is hard and challenging. Therefore, moms can be tempted to think they are wasting their time doing the mundane day-to-day responsibilities it takes to hold a family together.

I (Kathy) remember when the woman's liberation movement was on the rise in the 1970s. The impression I got as a young single woman was that child-rearing was an unwanted burden—that there was no joy, no fulfillment, and no significant purpose in it. This mindset still lingers to a degree with some women today. However, God does not want us to have that kind of an attitude toward raising children. In Israel's history, women longed to be mothers and considered barrenness a reproach and an affliction for which they cried out to God for help (cf., Rachel in Genesis 30:1, 22-23; Hannah in 1 Samuel 1:5-11). God answered their prayers by giving them children, and it was considered a great blessing that resulted in thankfulness and praise to God.

Mom, when you are tempted toward discouragement or overwhelmed by caring for the never-ending needs of your children, it would be helpful to remember what God's Word says. You can renew your mind with the following verses that emphasize the kindness of God in giving you children, and the attitude you should have toward motherhood and family overall.

> *He gives the barren woman a home, making her the joyous mother of children. Praise the LORD!*
> *Psalm 113:9*

> *Behold, children are a heritage from the Lord, the fruit of the womb a reward.*
> *Psalm 127:3*

These verses highlight the preciousness of children. They remind us that they are to be seen as a gift graciously given to us by God, not a burden to endure or escape. God desires that moms and dads have a pleasant countenance within the home because that's what makes a home a haven and a family that children will love to identify with.

3. Make your children feel like they are part of the "Team".

Another way parents can foster a sense of family identity is by making their children feel like they are part of the team. One of the most effective ways this can be done is by giving children household jobs to do that benefit the family. The purpose is not just to get things done around the house, but to also help them feel like they are needed and belong to the family. Not only will this foster a good work ethic (which is lacking today), but it conveys to your child, "We need you. You're a vital part of our family."

This should start as soon as your children are old enough to take on some type of responsibility that is appropriate for their age (it can usually start as early as age 3 or 4). Young children can take on a small chore that is their particular responsibility, and that will benefit the whole family. They can empty a small wastebasket in the bathroom when it is full, help set the dinner table, or help put away the silverware from the dishwasher. As children get older, they can be given greater responsibilities such as folding laundry or assisting in some type of yard work.

Furthermore, it will be essential to reinforce the significance of your child's contribution by saying something positive and encouraging, such as, "That helps us a lot. Thank you so much!" Alternatively you can say, "I don't think I could have done that without you," or "That would not have gotten done without you." Encouraging statements like these will give your child a sense that they are a vital part of the family.

Russell Moore wrote an insightful article about this titled, "Parenting and Work: Helping Our Children Gain a Sense of Belonging."[2] In the article, he states, "Work is a part of helping our children see where they fit in our family in order to gain a sense of belonging." When a family is sharing responsibility for the work of maintaining the home, it helps foster a strong family identity; each member feels some ownership in the family. It builds a sense of "we are in this together."

Our heavenly Father does the same with His family. He gives His children spiritual gifts to fulfill His work. In doing so, He provides us with a sense of belonging and contributing to the family of God: "*To each is given the manifestation of the Spirit for the common good*" (1 Corinthians 12:7; cf. Romans 12:3-8; Ephesians 4:7, 12-16). Giving young children household responsibilities will do the same.

Additionally, as your children get older, you can help them feel that they are a part of the team by allowing them to give input on some decisions that affect them. These might include such things as how to arrange or decorate their bedroom, offering ideas for meals, or help in planning a family vacation. Allowing children to give input not only promotes a sense of belonging, but it also gives the impression that we are a team, and your children are a vital part of that team.

Furthermore, you can foster a sense of family identity with family pictures and videos: a family portrait displayed in the home, photo albums, and videos of family activities. View them from time to time, reminiscing about family outings, events, and achievements. The old adage at work here is that *a picture is worth a thousand words.*

What are some ways you can foster a sense of family identity?

CHAPTER 3

Demonstrate an Ongoing Love as Husband and Wife

Ephesians 5 exhorts husbands three times to love their wives (verses 25, 28, and 33). In Titus 2:3-4, the older women are exhorted to train the younger women to love their husbands. Jesus said in John 13:34, "*A new commandment I give to you, that you love one another: just as I have loved you, you also are to love one another.*" Many marriages would be greatly enhanced by displaying the same selfless and sacrificial love Christ had for the church.

Dad and Mom, the greatest influence you will have on your children will not come in your role as a father and mother, but as a husband and wife. Your children want you to love each other. Children thrive on the demonstration of love between mom and dad. In contrast, they wither in a home where there is constant bickering and a lack of love.

A common mistake many husbands and wives make after they have a child is to be so focused on the child that they neglect to maintain their relationship with each other. A father and mother can be very active with their children, taking them to many activities, but nullify much of their efforts in cultivating a good family heritage, if they do not demonstrate an ongoing love as husband and wife. Therefore, do not put your marriage relationship on hold while raising your children. As important as the parent-child relationship is, the husband-wife relationship is even more so.

1. Make your marriage relationship the priority relationship.

Genesis 2:24 speaks of the priority of the marriage relationship. The man is exhorted to "*hold fast to his wife,*" and the two shall become "*one flesh.*"One flesh communicates deep intimacy. It speaks of a relationship that is to be stronger and closer than any other human relationship. Give your children a sense of confidence and security in knowing that mom and dad love each other and are firmly committed to one another. It brings stability to the whole family and gives children a sense of refuge.

At a small-group marriage Bible study, a man shared of a time when he gave his wife a hug in front of his 5-year-old daughter. As he hugged his wife, he casually looked down at his daughter and said, "Honey, I sure do love your mother." He was not expecting a reply from his daughter. However, she said something he thought was very profound and had a profound effect on him. She said, "Thank you."

One of the greatest gifts you can give your children is a quality marriage, where mom and dad relate to each other in loving and sacrificial ways: doing little acts of kindness for each other, caring for each other, encouraging one another, and scheduling time to be together—just the two of you. Not only will this set an example for your children to follow, but it will also contribute to the atmosphere in the home, making it a place where children want to belong.

Think about it from a child's perspective—how can a child have a sense of refuge in a home where dad and mom talk unkindly to each other and are living in a cold war? Children can sense if their parents love each other or not. They can sense if mom and dad are in a happy or unhappy marriage, whether there is concord or discord in the home.[3]

2. Enhancing marital oneness

> *"Therefore a man shall leave his father and his mother and hold fast to his wife,* ***and they shall become one flesh****"* (emphasis added)
> *Genesis 2:24,* (cf. Matthew 19:5; Mark 10:7-8; Ephesians 5:31)

Notice once again that marriage is described as a "*one flesh*" relationship. Many people assume that this is simply referring to the sexual union between a husband and wife. And, of course, it includes that, but it involves more than sexual relations. It refers to a *new status and a new union* between a husband and wife. They are now one in God's eyes.

Furthermore, the one-flesh union is meant to manifest itself in practical and tangible ways. God wants a husband and wife to grow in marital oneness; to experience a *deep connection* with each other in body and soul.

So, what does it take to *experience* marital oneness? Marital oneness is enhanced when a husband and wife *touch* (i.e., connect) in five significant areas. We want to offer some practical and tangible ways for a husband and wife to do so. It would be beneficial to evaluate your marriage relationship in light of them. In what areas would you say you are strong? What areas are you weak and need to grow?

Touching physically. By this, we are referring to cuddling, snuggling, hugging, holding hands, and sitting close together. All marriages need a large amount of tenderness and affection. Unfortunately, physical touch and affection seem to diminish after marriage.

Physical touch and affection create warmth and endearment in a relationship. For example, think of a newborn baby. What is a baby's first line of communication? Physical touch. If the baby starts crying, what does mom do? She picks up her baby and holds him near to her. Why? Because it creates warmth, endearment, and a place of refuge for the baby.

Physical touch should be a part of your daily lives as a husband and wife. Some simple and practical ways of doing so would include:

- Holding hands while praying, or at times while walking together.
- Kissing before you leave for work and separate for the day.
- Hugging when you come together again after work.
- A caring touch is good medicine when the other has had a hard day.

Touching emotionally. Emotional intimacy is enhanced when you appropriately respond to the ups and downs in your spouse's life. Romans 12:15 exhorts us to "*Rejoice with those who rejoice* *and weep with those who weep.*" If we are to connect this way with our fellow church members, then surely, even more so we should connect this way with our spouse. We once heard emotional closeness described like this: "Emotional closeness in marriage should be so deep that when one-person cries, the other tastes salt."

Additionally, emotional intimacy is enhanced when you encourage and build up one another. 1 Thessalonians 5:11 says, "*Therefore, encourage one another and build one another up.*" Some simple and practical ways of doing so would include:

- Verbalizing appreciation for his hard work.
- Verbalizing appreciation for her homemaking sacrifices.
- Expressing words of admiration for each other.
- Expressing words of grace and empathy when the other has had a stressful day.

Furthermore, emotional intimacy is enhanced by small acts of affection and thoughtfulness, such as an affectionate note, a hug, a shoulder massage, a little gift, or flowers. Romans 12:10 implores us to "*love one another with brotherly affection. Outdo one another in showing honor.*"

Touching mentally. You are touching mentally when you share what you are learning and reflect on various issues and topics together. It could be on a broad range of topics, such as:

- Newsworthy events.
- An article you read on a particular topic, such as nutrition, exercise, politics, finances, childrearing, etc.
- Something you read in the Bible.
- Things you are learning about life.

Unfortunately, after a few years of marriage, many couples stop touching mentally. Communication becomes limited to family business; who will take the kids somewhere or something that needs to be fixed around the house. A good exercise for a husband and wife to do occasionally is to get a copy of the same book, read it at the same pace, then discuss what you are learning as you read through it. This is touching mentally.

Additionally, you are touching mentally when you value the ideas and opinions of your spouse, and when you are willing to see a situation from your spouse's point of view.

Take the time and effort to discover what the other person thinks about various matters, and it will create closeness in this vital area of your lives.

Touching socially. This takes place when you spend time together—just the two of you–going out to eat; having a date night; going for a walk, etc. In other words, you are touching socially when you do things together. This may mean learning to enjoy some of the things that your spouse likes to do.

- For a wife, it may mean going to a sporting event with her husband.
- For a husband, it may mean going for a walk or shopping with his wife.
- It may mean taking an active interest in each other's hobbies.

Additionally, you are touching socially by interacting with friendships together. Common friends tend to draw a husband and wife together, while separate friends tend to pull a husband

and wife apart. Furthermore, close friendships are more beneficial with other couples that have similar beliefs and a desire to grow spiritually; that have the same values and concerns for their children; that have many of the same interests and are relatively fun and easy to be around.

Finally, you are touching socially by attending social and recreational activities *together* more than alone. Since time for recreation is generally scarce because of how busy we are, we need to try to spend as much of the time that we do have together. And, of course, it will mean supporting the interest and the activities of your children together—spending time with each other as a family.

As you choose to do things together, even things that are not your favorite activity, you will develop a sense of teamwork and camaraderie.

Touching spiritually. One of the ways you touch spiritually is when you pray together as husband and wife. If you do not pray together and do not know where to begin, let us suggest the *A.C.T.S. Prayer Model:*

> **A**doration: begin by exalting the Lord for who He is—His attributes, character, and nature(without any petitions).
>
> **C**onfession: confessing personal sins to God and receiving His forgiveness.
>
> **T**hanksgiving: thanking God for what He has or is doing for you and others.

Supplication: asking God for something, either for yourself or on behalf of someone else.

Another way to touch spiritually is, of course, to read and study the Bible together, and interact over spiritual truths that you are learning. It would be ideal to be in a weekly church Bible study together. As a result, you will naturally be sharing what the Spirit of God is teaching you. Make a natural practice of talking about the Lord and biblical truth at home.

Additionally, you are touching spiritually when you attend church together, and when you serve the Lord together in a ministry.

In conclusion, evaluate your marriage relationship in light of these five areas. Mark the areas where improvement is needed in your relationship. Talk together about how you can be purposeful in implementing needed change. It should be easy to see that if you implement these five areas of touching in your marriage relationship, it will promote oneness in the most significant areas of your lives. As a result, it will create an atmosphere in the home where your children will thrive and reflect on with fond memories.

CHAPTER 4

Nurture a Relationship with Your Children

Parents need to prioritize building a loving and devoted relationship with their children that displays care, concern, sacrifice, and a commitment to their good. This is the kind of relationship our heavenly Father has with His children. Unfortunately, some parents tend to think that parenting is all about disciplining or merely making sure that material needs for their children are provided. Of course, the discipline of children and provision for their physical and material needs are essential, but parenting is more than that. *It is about a relationship.* The parent-child relational experience and development is vital. We clearly see that now that our children are older and married. Next to our children loving and serving the Lord, our greatest joy is to have a loving and meaningful relationship with them.

In this final chapter on cultivating a spirit of belonging and connectedness in family relationships, we want to offer several practical ways of nurturing a relationship with your children that will leave a lasting legacy.

1. Maximize the four golden moments in your child's day.

Great parents make the most of key moments in a child's daily life. There are several significant occasions to consider:

The first golden moment is the waking up time. Greet your children with a smile and an affectionate tone when you see them first thing in the morning, welcoming them to a new day. This helps to set the tone for the day.

The second golden moment is the sending off time. This is when they are leaving for school. It can be a time for a brief prayer and sending them off with some happy and loving words.

The third golden moment is the regathering time. This is when everyone returns home for the day from school and work and gathers at the dinner table. Unfortunately, sharing meals together as a family can easily get lost amidst the demands of busy schedules with everyone running here and there to their next activity. When we let this happen, we are missing out on a golden moment of connecting as a family.

Since we all have to eat, mealtime is one of the most natural occasions for family togetherness and fellowship. We had many good discussions with our children during this time, and it enhanced our family relationships. We highly recommend that you make it a priority in your family life and a necessary part of everyone's schedule. If you develop the tradition of enjoyable conversation around the dinner table when your children are young, they will be more inclined to want to continue being a part of a scheduled mealtime when they become teenagers and their schedules are filled with various activities.

During this time, eliminate any digital distractions by keeping the TV off and holding all phone calls and smartphone use. Allow everyone the chance to share in the family discussion. You can start with a simple question to get a conversation started—"What was the most interesting thing you did today?" You can also use this as a time to plan family events or discuss spiritual matters. Remember, this is a golden moment. Therefore, make it about 30 minutes of relaxed, enjoyable family time.

The fourth golden moment is the lying down time. This, of course, is bedtime. Bedtime is one of the best times for communication with your child, and communication builds the relationship. It is also a good time to settle a child down by reading a bedtime story, praying for them, and saying, "I love you" with a kiss good night. After a long day, parents can feel weary and not take advantage of this golden moment. However, you will be glad you did and may find that this is a time when your children are the most tender and the most eager to speak and listen.

Being consistent in these four golden moments in a regular day will do more for the relationship with your children than one or two major events in a year.

2. Write an occasional note to each child.

This is a small and simple gesture that communicates to your child that you are thinking of them. It is extra special when Dad writes a note because this is something that Mom usually does. It does not have to be a long note, just a simple sentence or two will do. For example:

- "I love you!"
- "Jesus loves you."
- "I'm so thankful to God that you are my son/daughter."
- "Hope you have an awesome day today."
- "Let's go for ice cream after dinner!"

Additionally, a note would be affirming when you see a positive characteristic emerging in your child. For example, you might point out the generosity or kindness your child showed to someone, or how well they did in a particular task. And, of course, an encouraging note from mom and dad would be timely when your child is facing something difficult.

Leave the note on the kitchen counter before you leave for work or put it in their school backpack, so when they are at school, they will see mom or dad's note. You can also write something on a sticky note and place it on their mirror or dresser. The time invested in a small note like this is only about 60 seconds. However, it will go far in nurturing the relationship with your children.

3. Attend your children's extracurricular activities.

It is important to show an interest in what your children are involved in (e.g., school events, athletic games, plays, band concerts, etc.). Ask questions about their activities and interests. In fact, it would be beneficial, whenever possible, for every family member to attend each other's events. Be a family that supports and celebrates each other. It will foster a sense of family identity and connectedness.

4. Follow through with promises and commitments.

"But you promised," are words that have spilled out in hurt and frustration from the mouths of countless children. One of the most hurtful things for a child is for a promise to be broken, especially by Mom or Dad. It can be a temptation for busy, distracted, or tired parents to flippantly make promises to their children that are forgotten just as quickly, or not follow through on promises because something else has come up. As the string of broken promises and commitments gets longer and longer, children will begin to view their parents with bitterness and resentment (cf. Ephesians 6:4a; Colossians 3:21).

Some time back, a young lady sought counsel from us on a family matter. It had to do with her father. He frustrated her and her siblings when they were young children by making promises and commitments but not following through with them. It did not create a good family heritage. Instead, it created animosity in the children against their father that had to be dealt with in later years.

Be alert to the promises you make to your children. Do not flippantly throw out promises that are forgotten just as quickly. This frustrates children and weakens the relationship. How much trust and confidence can a child have in a parent who does not keep their promises? Trust is essential for a healthy and thriving parent-child relationship. James 5:12 exhorts, "*Let your 'yes' be yes and your 'no' be no, so that you may not fall under condemnation.*"

Our heavenly Father keeps His promises. We can believe in God's promises and place confidence that He will fulfill them, and He exhorts us to do the same with the promises we make to our children (cf. Hebrews 10:23; 11:11).

5. Make eye contact when your child is talking to you.

Did you ever try talking to someone who would not make eye contact with you? They just kept looking in another direction or at their smartphone? How did it make you feel? Most likely you felt trivial, like what you had to say was not very important.

Children measure love by our attentiveness to them. When one of our children tries to communicate with us, we show the importance of what they have to say by establishing eye contact and giving them our undivided attention. Most of the time, children only need a few minutes of our full attention. However, many parents are often too caught up in other matters to listen and focus on what their children have to say. Even when we are relaxing we can be distracted by our smartphones, social media, Internet browsing, or TV. As a result, if one of our children tries to talk to us about something, there is no eye contact, we stay focused on what we are doing, and they get the impression that they are not very important.

Now, of course, there will be times we cannot stop what we are doing and give our child our full attention. Children do need to learn that they cannot always interrupt if there is something important that we are doing, or when we are in a conversation with someone. However, if this is a consistent pattern (due to over-busyness, inattentiveness, or pre-occupation), our children will get the feeling that they are bothersome and that we are not very interested in their world, and it will impede the relationship. For the most part, we need to stop what we are doing and focus on them when they want to talk to us. This should begin at a very early age. An open relationship between teen-agers and their parents (where they communicate freely and openly), is a dynamic that has been cultivated over the years, not something that just begins at age sixteen.

Parents need to be active listeners, not passive listeners, even to very young children. Ephesians 6:4 exhorts, "*Father's do not provoke your children to anger.*" Onc of the ways we can provoke our children to anger is by not being attentive when they are trying to communicate with us. Focused attention demonstrates love and respect to a child; that you really care and value your interaction with them. It will nurture the relationship and convey that what you think they have to say is important and that you are interested in their world and activities. As a result, they will be more inclined to communicate with you in the future.

6. Allow honest, open dialogue and appeal.

Strong and healthy relationships will have open lines of communication, where all family members feel heard and respected. Unfortunately, many children feel as though they cannot approach their parents with struggles, concerns, or disagreements. Too often, parents continue to view their children as being too young to think for themselves or feel threatened by decisions their children make that may be different than their own. By not attempting to listen and understand our children's perspective, we may give them the impression that we are insensitive to their thoughts and feelings. This type of family atmosphere and interaction will hinder a spirit of connectedness between family members.

As children grow (especially into their teen years), they should be shown the respect of being allowed to engage their parents in mature disagreement, appeal, and discussion. In order for children to feel the freedom to do this, parents will need to be approachable, allowing open and honest dialogue. James 3:17 states that a wise person is "*open to reason.*"

We needed to apply this at times with our children, but one time in particular stands out. At the age of 16, our son, Armand, said that he wanted to learn to play the drums. He and a group of guys in our church youth group wanted to start a youth band, and he wanted to be the drummer. There was an exceptionally gifted 19-year old in the youth group who recently came to faith in Christ. He was a prodigy who played several instruments and was able to write songs and music, and he was going to lead this band and write Christian songs.

Well, needless to say, the songs were a little weak theologically, and they would often add a loud, piercing scream in some of their songs. That was a bit hard for us to handle, and it became a topic of discussion in our home. We tried to balance our guidance with grace, and not overreact in a strict pharisaical way and rob our son and the band members of their joy. They really believed in their hearts that they were serving the Lord and getting the Gospel message out to unbelievers their age.

We continued to have many conversations about it and tried to coach him. We were able to agreeably disagree in some matters while coming to an agreement in others, *and not sacrifice the relationship.* As a result, it enhanced our relationship because our son felt that we were willing to listen to his perspective even if we did not completely agree. Two verses in Proverbs 18 speak to this:

A fool takes no pleasure in understanding,
but only in expressing his opinion.
Proverbs 18:2

If one gives an answer before he hears, it is his folly and shame.
Proverbs 18:13

When we are approachable, we are displaying Christ-like wisdom and humility to our children. In instances where we do disagree, we model godliness by showing them how to disagree graciously and humbly with those who do not see things the way we do. This is a skill that our children will need to have as they approach their teen years and especially in adulthood.

Eventually, our son's band moved beyond that scream and became a great worship band. Several of them still use their musical talent for the Lord on Sunday mornings at our church.

Your children need to know that they do not have to be afraid to approach you with open and honest dialogue over a disagreement, or something they may be struggling with, or something culturally they are thinking through without mom and dad overreacting in anger, intimidation, military-style, or a lecture. Lord willing, this will leave a legacy your children will appreciate and apply in their own children-rearing years.

What are some ways you can nurture a relationship with your children?

Essential Element 2

Sow Seeds that Reap Cherished Family Memories

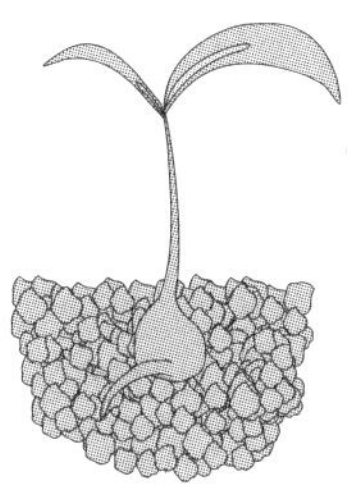

It was one of those hot summer days when many families from surrounding towns decided to spend the afternoon at the beach. The sun was shining and bright, the air was hot and humid, and the water was cool and refreshing. Umbrellas and towels were spread out along the beach. Young children were splashing in the shallow water with their moms and dads nearby. Some of the older children were building sandcastles, and a group of teens started a beach volleyball game. The parents who brought their families to the beach for the day were probably only looking for a way to cool off and have some fun and relaxation on a hot Saturday afternoon. They may not have even been aware that they were also doing one of the most important jobs of parenting—making memories.

Earlier, we referred to the memorials that God gave to Israel and the Church. Those memorials were meant to aid a person's memory in preserving what is most cherished and provide a sense of solidarity and unity. They included festivals, monuments, the Lord's Supper, and growing relationships with brothers and sisters in Christ. The ability to remember and recall past events and experiences is a gift graciously given to us from God. Therefore, as it relates to family, we want to be purposeful in cultivating good memories.

Proverbs 24:3-4 speaks of rooms in a home being "*filled with all precious and pleasant riches*" — implying a blessed family life. One of the things that the most cherished and satisfying relationships have in common is happy memories. Think about your childhood. What memories fill your mind when you think back? For some, it may be delightful memories, but for others, it may be painful. The point is to consider the kind of memories you want your children to have, and to be purposeful in creating precious and pleasant ones. You only have your children at home for a season of life. So how can you build good memories that will cause them to look back affectionately?

In this section, we will consider two ways parents can accomplish this:

- Make home a fun place to live
- Create and enjoy family traditions

CHAPTER 5

Make Home a Fun Place to Live

If you saw the movie, "The Sound of Music," you will recall Georg Von Trapp as the widowed father of six children. He is portrayed as a detached disciplinarian, keeping his six children under strict control. He would blow a whistle and his children would stand at attention and march in and out of his presence like an army platoon. But when their new nanny, Maria, became a part of the family, she brought fun and laughter into their lives. Fun and laughter changed the atmosphere of the home from a boot camp to a fun place to be.

Fun should be an essential ingredient for families. What follows are some ways that parents can cultivate an enjoyable atmosphere that makes the home a fun place to live.

1. Slow down.

How does slowing down help make the home a fun place to live? First, it allows you time to enjoy spontaneity. We are unable to be spontaneous when every minute of our day is filled with something. However, when we make a determined effort to slow our lives down by limiting commitments and additional responsibilities, especially during the child-rearing years, we gain the fun that spontaneity can bring. Our kids loved it when a friend's mom would call and ask, "Do you want to meet at the playground for lunch?" or dad would say, "Let's go get an ice cream cone." We were able just to drop everything and go! That can only happen when your days are unhindered by excessive obligations that pull you away from the family.

If you feel like your life leaves little room for spontaneity, take some time to evaluate what is consuming your life (or your child's life) that could either be eliminated or cut back so that you would have more free time. Make a renewed commitment to live a slower-paced life where your days are not consumed with out-of-the-ordinary responsibilities, or driving the kids to endless lessons and activities that push the family apart and create a tense and stressful atmosphere.

Slowing down also enables you to enjoy today. It has been said that the best way to make it through the child-rearing years is to grin and bear it until it gets better. However, joy and memory-making are sacrificed when our focus is on merely "making it through the child-rearing years." While the parenting years can, at times, be filled with stress and activities, they are years that will not last forever. Therefore, slow down and be mindful to enjoy this period of life. Seek to prioritize the things that matter most. Get on the floor and build that block tower for the fiftieth time. Read that same story for the hundredth time. Play hide and seek over and over again, watch that Jenga tower collapse again, play Barbie with your daughter once more, and make countless batches of Play-Doh cookies—all in an effort to slow down and love on your kids! Do it today, because one day things will change, and the things you miss enjoying today with your children cannot be recaptured again tomorrow.

2. Bring humor and laughter into the home.

While every parent must take their God-given role seriously, humor and laughter have a way of bonding family members together and developing family cohesion. Additionally, they create memories that are recalled and talked about for years to come. Again, Proverbs 17:22 reminds us that "*A joyful heart is good medicine"* (a cure for the body as well as the emotions), *but a crushed spirit dries up the bones"*(it saps a person's vitality). Often, as parents, we can become so overwhelmed by the pressures and responsibilities of life that it can rob us of our joy, cast a dark cloud on the atmosphere in the home, and render the family unenjoyable. Humor and laughter will ease the strain that is part of the parenting years, and create a more pleasant home atmosphere. And besides, children love to see mom and dad being light-hearted, smiling, and laughing. Laughter not only encourages your own spirit, but it refreshes the hearts of those around you.

We are thankful for the ways the Lord has helped us to incorporate laughter and humor into our home. To be sure, we did take our parenting seriously, especially when it came to dealing with our children's heart attitudes and behavior. However, we also had a desire for our children to see that mom and dad can also be fun; that we were not overly rigid; that we laugh at things that are funny; that wc have a balance between the serious and the humorous. The Lord gave us many opportunities to demonstrate this to our children.

I (Kathy) remember, for example, a time when we were driving home from a family vacation, and we had about a six-hour drive ahead of us. About halfway home, we stopped at a rest area that had a novelty shop. There was something in that store that our son wanted—a whoopee cushion! He was about 10 years old at the time. Well, I have to admit, I initially thought to myself, "Is it okay to let him have something like that? He's the pastor's son! What would people think? And, it might encourage some unfavorable behavior." Well, we decided to let him get it, and we are so glad we did. We busted a gut laughing as it occupied us the rest of the drive home. And in the weeks to follow, it brought laughter and fun into our home. Eventually, he lost it. But what did not get lost was the fond memory of how a whoopee cushion helped to bring laughter into our home and make it a fun place to live.

The next point will expand on this, but first, we want to give you a word of caution. Be careful to distinguish between healthy humor and ridicule, sarcasm, or excessive teasing. Healthy humor and laughter can bring healing and lighten up the atmosphere in a home. Conversely, ridicule, sarcasm, and excessive teasing can wound.

3. Do fun things together.

You have heard the old saying, "All work and no play makes Jack a dull boy." We can also say, "All work and no fun makes for a dull family life." Family relationships tend to stagnate when the routine of the daily grind sets in. It is obvious that if we want to leave good memories with our children, then we must invest time doing fun things *together*. Families that have fun together have a strong spirit of family identity and connectedness.

Parents who feel that they have not had many happy childhood memories may feel hampered in building happy memories for their own children. If you do not have a lot of happy memories of your own to pass on to your children, you may need to borrow memory-building ideas from others. Find out what others do and implement them in your own family.

Breaking out of the daily routine does not have to be expensive or extravagant. What follows is a starter list of ideas we have compiled, and we want to encourage you to add some of your own ideas to it. Notice how they emphasize the importance of spending time together as a family. Spending time with someone deepens the relationship and creates memories, and so it is with family relationships.

4. Sixty-five memory building ideas.

- Camp out as a family.
- Walking, hiking, or bicycling together.
- Explore Metro Parks. (In fact, Metro Parks generally have monthly lists of activities for the whole family to participate in. You can get a monthly list of family activities online or at a Metro Park office).
- Pick fruit at a farm.
- Go on a fall hayride and pick out some pumpkins.

- Create a family scrapbook of memorable events.
- Have a family movie night. Take the children to the store to pick out some snacks. (However, do not let watching movies or TV be your "go-to" family activity).
- Take some type of lessons together as a family. (i.e., tennis, volleyball, golf, karate).
- Work a long-term project together. (Tinker with an old car; build something; paint something; create something!)

- Trade places at the dinner table with each family member acting like the person who usually sits there.

- Take the family out to a Saturday breakfast or brunch.
- Let the kids plan a family event.
- Plan a mystery trip and surprise a family member.
- Take a (clean) joke book out from the library.
- Play family board games.

- Have nerf gun battles.
- Designate a special day with each child, other than birthdays. (For example, you might say, "Anna, this Saturday is going to be your special day. What can we do as a family that you would enjoy doing?")
- Occasionally, do something spontaneous (Some of the best memories come from unexpected, spontaneous times).
- Develop a family book of humor, writing down funny things the children did and said when they were little.
- Make cookies using an illustrative recipe.

- Set up a backyard obstacle course and time each other.
- Play balloon ball by hitting balloons back and forth with your hands.
- Hide a "treasure" and then make clues for someone to find it.
- Learn to make flowers out of tissue paper.

- Take turns telling a silly story, each person adding a sentence.
- Purchase a yearly membership to the zoo, an amusement park, an Arboretum, or a museum so you can visit often.

- Build a tent with blankets or set-up an actual tent inside the home and sleep there.
- Spread out butcher paper and draw a city.
- Glue cardboard boxes together and make buildings. (You could even paint them).
- Attach ribbons to a stick and then dance with it.
- Thread macaroni on yarn to make a necklace and paint it.

- Draw chalk outlines of each other on the driveway, then color them in.
- Hunt for smooth rocks and paint them.
- Go on a color scavenger hunt and take pictures of things that have the color of the rainbow.
- Paint with homemade finger paint.
- Find somewhere comfy and listen to an audio book.

- Search online for dot-to-dot and print them out to finish.
- Learn to fold paper airplanes, newspaper hats, or origami-jumping frogs.
- Have a backyard campfire on a cool evening, cooking hotdogs and marshmallows.
- Tell stories of something one of the kids did way back when.
- Have a Play-Doh-creating contest with some friends. (Have Dad be the judge).

- Make puppets out of brown paper bags.
- Make colorful crayon rubbings of different kinds of leaves.
- Draw squares on the driveway with chalk and play two square or four square.
- Write a letter to a friend and mail it.

- Put hula-hoops in the yard and play Frisbee golf.
- Cut up small pieces of colored paper and make a design with them.
- Have a Lego building contest with friends. (Have a neighbor be the judge).

- Draw a giant hopscotch on the driveway with chalk.
- Work on a puzzle together.
- Have a picnic in the backyard.
- Jump rope. (Look up some jump rope rhymes online).
- Skype or FaceTime with grandparents or cousins.

- Set up a mini-golf course in the house or backyard.
- Make a snowman.
- Join a reading club at the library.
- Wash the car.
- Color or paint paper doilies from the dollar store.

- Make an obstacle course on the driveway and ride your bike through it.
- Play a fun joke on Mom or Dad.
- Sing and make music together—create a family songbook.
- Have the kids act out a play or a story from the Bible.
- Make some homemade presents to give away.
- Color or paint some pictures and pass them out at a nursing home.
- Pack a picnic lunch and meet some friends at the park.
- Read a book together as a family.

As mentioned, this list is not meant to be exhaustive. It is simply meant to give you some ideas and to stimulate you to think of some of your own ideas. There are a multitude of ways to spend time together as a family. Do not let the years slip by without creating some memorable times that your children will cherish when they are adults, and perhaps pass on to their own children someday. Use your creativity to think of things that will work for your family. But understand that the real memory-builder is not necessarily found in the sum total of all these things or any one of them by itself. *The real memory-builder is in experiencing these things together as a family.*

CHAPTER 6

Create and Enjoy Family Traditions

Another meaningful way in which we can strengthen our family and sow cherished memories is by creating family traditions. Traditions are customary or unique ways in which a family performs a routine and a family's unique way of celebrating special occasions. Every family should be diligent in developing and perpetuating traditions. Not only do they give a sense of solidarity to a family, but children also look forward to them in anticipation. This generally comes naturally by how we celebrate birthdays, Mother's and Father's Day, the Christian holidays of Christmas and Easter, as well as national holidays such as Memorial Day, Independence Day, and Thanksgiving. However, "ordinary day" traditions are also important since we live most of our lives in ordinary days. Therefore, when establishing family traditions, it is helpful to not only think in terms of yearly traditions that come naturally from major holidays, but also weekly, and even daily. They can benefit families in several ways.

1. **Family traditions are anchor points in an ever-changing world.**

It seems as though life is continually changing. Many things can throw us off balance. Traditions provide an essential constant in family life. They help keep us grounded.

Consider implementing a simple daily tradition that becomes a way of life for your family—something that strengthens family identity and allows all family members to connect each day. For example, it can be a bedtime routine of reading a story and ending the day praying, thanking God for the day. Some adults look back on their childhood with fond memories when mom or dad would read bedtime stories to them each evening. Consider making daily meals an enjoyable tradition of gathering together as a family to enjoy food and purposeful conversation (without electronic devices). Sharing a meal together daily as a family has a positive influence on children. Others look back at evening walks they had with their parents. Evening walks are a great time to have a relaxing discussion. One family we knew loved to sing. They would sing a song in the evening before going to bed. These daily anchor-points in the life of your family will give children a sense of stability and familiarity. Some of the fondest childhood memories are borne out of these ordinary-day traditions.

2. Family traditions strengthen our bond as a family unit.

Life today is so fast-paced and demanding, pulling us in many different directions, so it is vital to find ways to reconnect with each other. Establishing family traditions helps us do just that. Family traditions allow us to slow down in our whirlwind world and connect as a family. There is value in establishing certain family traditions just for the sake of spending time together as a family. Children develop warm feelings as they remember special times together. They provide cohesion to the nuclear family, drawing children closer to their parents, siblings, and extended family members.

I (Armand) come from a line of full-blooded Italians. One trait about most Italians is that we are passionate about family traditions. Often our traditions are passed down from generation to generation, and they become a part of the rhythm of life. Every Sunday, during my childhood years, all my aunts, uncles, and cousins (and there were many!) would gather together at Nano and Nana's house. We would enjoy Nana's homemade pasta, sauce, and Italian bread, as well as family interaction (very loud interaction!). That weekly tradition still holds a special place in my heart. I cherish the memories that were created during that time.

Consider implementing a weekly family tradition that draws the family together. Sometimes a family tradition can be as simple as a Sunday spaghetti dinner after church with everyone gathered around the table in relaxed conversation. Some families implement a weekly theme, such as Sunday Sundaes, Taco Tuesday, Friday Pizza (or Popcorn) Movie Night, Saturday Morning Pancake Breakfast, Saturday Board Game Night, or a Sunday afternoon walk. Weekly routines like these not only create fond memories for young children, but they also foster a sense of family identity and connectedness. It shows children that their family prioritizes interpersonal interactions and experiences. In the end, preserving and nurturing family traditions will help draw you closer to those you love, and in turn, cultivate a good family heritage.

3. Family traditions are opportunities to remember God's goodness and faithfulness.

An essential part of Israel's traditional celebrations was to remember what God had done for them. They were meant to celebrate His goodness and faithfulness and instill in their children a sense of their spiritual heritage (Exodus 12:12-14; 13:8-10). For us as Christians, the yearly celebrations that come naturally with the Christian holidays of Christmas and Easter are wonderful opportunities for us to do the same. Since Christmas and Easter have been secularized and commercialized, fewer and fewer people understand their true meaning. Furthermore, we can easily get caught up in the hustle and bustle of these holidays along with everyone else and lose sight of their meaning. Therefore, we need to be more proactive in communicating their true meaning to our children. As we observe the biblical meaning of Christmas and Easter to our children, we give them a clear understanding of God's provision for our salvation. Music, visual aids, decorations, family activities, special church services, sharing the love of Christ with the less fortunate, and the various plans and events that accompany these Christian holidays can make communicating their truth to our children joyous, meaningful, and unforgettable.

Christmas is a special time for children. When our children were young, we began to implement the yearly Christmas tradition called "The Waiting Tree" (waiting for the coming of Christ), which is similar to the popular Jesse Tree used today.[4] This was an excellent way for our children to learn the biblical background of Christmas. This large felt tree was placed on our refrigerator on the first day of December. Each day, from December 1st to the 25th, our children would take turns placing a small felt object on the tree that represented the people, prophesies, or events leading up to the birth of Jesus Christ. This was done after Dad read the appropriate Scripture that related to the prophecy or event, ending on Christmas Day with the reading of the Christmas story in Luke 2:1-21. This yearly tradition was a wonderful way to enhance our children's Christmas focus—remembering God's faithfulness in sending us the Savior.

Easter is the Christian's Fourth of July. It is a day to celebrate the most significant event in human history—the resurrection of Jesus Christ! It became a tradition in our home to greet one another on Easter morning with the salutation, "Christ is risen!" while the others responded, "He is risen indeed!" Easter church worship service was always an extra-special highlight of the day. Following our church service, we would head to Aunt Mary's house (Kathy's sister) for dinner. Traditionally, before dinner was served, our niece Becca would read the resurrection story followed by Uncle Dan praying and thanking God for life everlasting that has been offered to us through Christ.

Of course, many different family traditions can help commemorate the meaning of Easter. Some families have a tradition of wearing new clothes on Easter as a way of signifying new life through the resurrection of Jesus Christ. Similarly, as a way of teaching the death, burial, and resurrection of Jesus Christ, some families plant seeds in a flower bed each year. In John 12:24, Jesus speaks about a seed needing to be planted and die in order to bring forth an abundant harvest: *"Truly, truly, I say to you, unless a grain of wheat falls into the earth and dies, it remains alone; but if it dies, it bears much fruit."* Jesus is that seed. As beautiful flowers begin to grow, it becomes a good object lesson of the resurrection of Christ, bringing new life to many.

4. Family traditions pass on a national heritage to our children.

Memorial Day and *Independence Day* are national holidays and opportunities to instill in our children a sense of patriotism.

Many young people enjoy cookouts, parades, and fireworks on these days, but few know what all the celebrating is about. Memorial Day is a day to honor the men and women who have given their lives for our civil liberties while serving in the military. Independence Day celebrates the birth of our nation and freedom from tyranny. Therefore, amidst the cookouts with family and friends, it would be fitting to pause and take some time to recognize the original essence of these holidays. This is part of instilling in our children a sense of their national heritage. It is similar to the way the Israelites passed on their national heritage to their children through the meaning of the Passover. Some families visit a local or national cemetery on Memorial Day and place flags or flowers on the graves of fallen soldiers.

Thanksgiving Day provides a wonderful opportunity to practice a yearly tradition that promotes memories of predictable smells that are associated with family togetherness. The turkey roasting in the oven, apple pie, and brewing cider can breed aromas that lead one's thoughts to special family times together. More importantly, this day provides the perfect opportunity to spend time thanking God for His faithfulness, goodness, and blessings. Before the big meal, dad can briefly tell the story of the Pilgrims seeking religious freedom or read William Bradford's "First Thanksgiving Proclamation."

Our son-in-law, Mike, began a special Thanksgiving tradition with our family. Each family member is to be prepared to share a short testimony of what they were most thankful for this past year. After dinner, we gather in the comfortable atmosphere of the family room, and each of us would share a testimony of thanksgiving to God. Then Mike would play his guitar, leading us in a song of praise. It is a precious time for our family, a witness to our children and grandchildren of God's faithfulness, and a time to glorify Him with hearts of praise and thanksgiving!

5. Family traditions come in all shapes and sizes.

Family traditions can include a particular way to celebrate birthdays, Mother's Day, and Father's Day. They can consist of annually attending major league baseball home openers, berry picking every summer, a fall hayride that ends with hot chocolate, making Christmas cookies with the kids, or an annual family ride to see Christmas lights, etc. We know of a family with seven children that has a yearly Bocce Ball tournament where they invite friends to participate. It has grown to be a fun and cherished event with many friends and family attending.

Family traditions can serve as opportunities to pass on family history and culture to the next generation. We feel connected to our ancestors when we engage in the traditions that our families have practiced for generations. It may be a secret family food recipe that Great Grandma brought over from the "old country," or a distinctive family saying, greeting, or story passed down through the generations. Additionally, you can make use of modern technology by recording Grandma and Grandpa's testimony of their conversion to Christ to share with your children when they grow older.

Family traditions can include watching family videos and viewing pictures on New Year's Day that reflect family events that took place the past year. Fortunately, our daughter-in-law, Roxana, is a photographer and videographer and sees the importance of capturing these special moments! These pictures and videos remind us of what we have been through together (an essential aspect of family identity).

Cherished family memories and traditions are among our most precious possessions. As simple as some of them may be, nevertheless, they create fond memories for our children. That is why we should be thoughtful and diligent in sowing them into the lives of our children. With a little imagination and preparation, family traditions can become family treasures.

Essential Element 3

Instill Biblical Truth and Values into the Lives of Your Children

Patrick Henry, one of the founding fathers of the United States of America, describes the spiritual inheritance he wanted to leave his children. In his Last Will and Testament, he wrote,

> "I have now disposed of all my property to my family. There is one thing more I wish I could give them, and that is the Christian Religion. If they had that and I had not given them one shilling, they would be rich; and if they had not that and I had given them all the world, they would be poor indeed."[5]

If we, as parents, simply focus on a material inheritance or even many of the things we have mentioned so far in this book, but leave out this aspect — a spiritual inheritance — our children would be poor indeed. The most important part of the education of our children is that they are taught to think and live according to the eternal truths and values presented in God's Word. If parents do not teach their children biblical truths and values, the world will teach them lies and worldly values.

How can parents instill a spiritual heritage in their children? Deuteronomy 6 gives parents guidance and a wise pattern to follow. Referring to God's Word, it says,

> *And these words that I command you today shall be on your heart. You shall teach them diligently to your children, and shall talk of them when you sit in your house, and when you walk by the way, and when you lie down, and when you rise.*
>
> *Deuteronomy 6:6-7*

There are two vitally important implications to observe in this exhortation. *First, notice that the emphasis for the responsibility of children's biblical instruction is on the parents, not the religious leaders.* Parents are called by God to pass on a spiritual heritage to their children. Unfortunately, too many parents seem to be content to merely delegate this responsibility to the local church or Christian school. Though valuable, pastors, Sunday School teachers, and Christian school teachers are supplemental to the child's spiritual development. The primary source of biblical instruction and the spiritual development of children is the parents. This is made clear, not only in this passage in Deuteronomy, but also in Proverbs: *"Hear, my son, your father's instruction, and forsake not your mother's teaching" (Proverbs 1:8; see also 2:1; 3:1; 4:1; 5:1; 6:1; 7:1), and Ephesians 6:4: "Fathers, do not provoke your children to anger, but bring them up in the discipline and instruction of the Lord."*

Second, it is crucial to notice that parents teach their children in two ways: by example and verbal instruction. Deuteronomy 6:6 begins by saying that God's Word *"shall be on your (the parents) heart."* It is so important that parents *not only* teach their children how to live in a God-honoring way *but also* show them by example. To accomplish this, parents must maintain a personal relationship with the Lord that is alive, active, and growing — striving, by God's grace, to live out the truths they are commending to their children. As a result, the children will see biblical truth lived out before their eyes and be more inclined toward practicing the same thing in their own life.

Additionally, Deuteronomy 6:7 exhorts, *"Teach them diligently to your children."* Verbal instruction of God's Word was to be done diligently and regularly: *"When you sit in your house, and when you walk by the way, and when you lie down, and when you rise."* The general idea behind this verse is that biblical instruction in the family should be a way of life. It should be part of the natural activity of everyday life. Parents ought to be cultivating a biblical and God-oriented worldview in their children.

We want to emphasize, once again, that helping children apply the Christian faith to everyday life is a balance of modeling and teaching. Parents have a greater influence on the next generation than anyone else.

Keeping this in mind, in this section we want to consider:

- The sacred purpose of the family
- The means parents are to use for instructing children
- Nine essential life lessons to teach your children

CHAPTER 7

The Sacred Purpose of the Family

God's sacred purpose for the family is to perpetuate a legacy of faith that honors Him. Of course, there are many other wonderful things family life provides, but this is the overall purpose. As parents, you have been given the high calling of nurturing your children's trust in God, and to construct a solid foundation upon which they can do the same for their children and their children's children after them.

Let's consider some indispensable ways parents can accomplish this.

1. Make Christ and His cause the priority in your family.

Only one life, 'twill soon be past,
Only what's done for Christ will last.

That has long been one of Armand's favorite sayings. Our children have heard him recite it on many occasions during their growing-up years. In fact, they each have a plaque on the wall of their homes with this saying on it.

Christian moms and dads must always keep in mind an essential biblical truth—as important as the family is, *the family should not be viewed as an end in itself.* Your family does not exist merely and solely for itself. It exists for something greater—greater than family functions, family gatherings, sports, and other events. Ultimately, it exists for Christ and His cause. As Jesus says, "*Seek first the kingdom of God and his righteousness*" (Mathew 6:33).

Although the institution of marriage and the family has a vital place in God's purposes for humanity in our present age, Jesus places a perimeter on its overall significance by placing it in the broader context of the kingdom of God. We do not live to glorify the family. The family lives to glorify God. We are to make Christ and His cause the highest priority in life, and this includes family life. Ephesians 1:9-10 gives us the big picture of God's overall purpose for humanity (including families): *"Making known to us the mystery of his will, according to his purpose, which he set forth in Christ as a plan for the fullness of time, to unite all things in him, things in heaven and things on earth."* This establishes Jesus Christ as the focal point of God's end-time purposes and is the reason why Christian marriages and families must be committed to Christ and His cause.

It's always sad to see some Christian families become so focused on the family itself or extra-curricular activities that they stop involvement in the local church (God's ordained institution to carry out His purposes). This happens when we view the family as an end in itself. Make Christ and His cause the focal point of your family. If you are not intentional in this, other extra-curricular activities will inadvertently squeeze this priority out of your family life. As shepherds of your children, you will need to make sure that other activities are not hindering a love for Christ and His cause. Show your children the priority you place on Sunday worship, Christian service, prayer, Bible study, and a burden for the spiritually lost and hurting. This is a vital and precious heritage that parents must pass on to their children.

2. Display an authentic Christianity at home.

One thing we have observed over the years is that hypocrites make bad parents. "Do as I say, not as I do" is not a workable parenting plan. Why would a 13-year old son want to walk in the ways of the Lord if his 40-year old father is not walking in the ways of the Lord? If a mother seems to get along fine without an apparent dependence on God, why would an 11-year old daughter be concerned about God in daily life?

The longstanding adage is true: "Some things are better caught than taught." One of the most important things you can do is set a godly example for your children. If you want your children to be honest and truthful, then you must be honest and truthful. If you want them to have an authentic relationship with the Lord, show them what that looks like. Again, not only are we to instruct our children in the ways of the Lord, but we must also be an example to follow. Proverbs 23:26 says, *"My son, give me your heart, and let your eyes observe my ways."* Parents, by God's grace, must aspire to embody the biblical values and virtues they are commending to their children. We must ask ourselves some sobering questions: "How is my walk with the Lord and my growth in Christ-likeness? What kind of model and testimony do my children observe from me at home?"

You cannot have a disconnect in your walk with the Lord from what you are at church to what you are at home, or your children will most likely not embrace the things of God. You will be a stumbling block to their faith and turn them off to spiritual realities. Nothing will make biblical truth more distasteful to a child than hypocritical or spiritually shallow parents. If following Christ is just a dull ho-hum existence, then our children will observe this and be confused. Actually, the pleasure, joy, and peace of God should define our countenance and attitudes toward life. It is vital that our children see this reality. It will provide an atmosphere in the home where faith can grow, and prayerfully, leave a lasting legacy your children will carry into adulthood.

Of course, no parent is perfect. We will all fall short at times. However, even times of failure and sin can be opportunities to display authentic Christianity in the home. For example, there may be an occasion when you sinfully lose your temper with one of your children and say something demeaning. When this happens, it would be appropriate to ask forgiveness from your child, saying,"I'm sorry. I should not have gotten angry like that and said what I said. It was a sin against God and you. I was wrong. Will you please forgive me?" Your child will be blessed by receiving an honest confession, and it will model an example for them to follow. Contrition is caught as well as taught. Your confession will show your children that you value their feelings and accept responsibility for your sins against them and God. Prayerfully, this too will be a legacy your children will follow into adulthood when they have children of their own.

3. Pray for your children.

Raising a child is a huge undertaking with tremendous responsibility. We all feel a sense of inadequacy for the task, which drives us to prayer, calling out to God. Prayer expresses our dependence on God. Prayer recognizes that there is an element of spiritual warfare in raising children in the discipline and instruction of the Lord (Ephesians 6:1-4, 10-18). You will find that some of your best parenting happens when you are humbly bent on your knees before God.

First and foremost, pray for their salvation. Since the Bible teaches that *"Salvation belongs to the LORD"* (Jonah 2:9; Revelation 7:10), pray that God will work a work of grace in the heart of your children; that He will draw their hearts to Jesus. Ask God to open their spiritual eyes and ears to the glorious truth of the Gospel; that they would come to recognize that they are sinners in need of the Savior; that they would repent of their sins and place saving faith in the atoning work of Christ on the cross. Pray this regularly from the moment of their birth. God wants us to be vigilant in faith, believing that the power of the Gospel can reach the heart of our children.

> *For I am not ashamed of the gospel, for it is the power of God for salvation to everyone who believes, to the Jew first and also to the Greek. For in it the righteousness of God is revealed from faith for faith, as it is written, "The righteous shall live by faith."*
>
> *Romans 1:16-17*

Of course, your child's conversion is only the beginning. Pray for their spiritual growth and maturity. One recommendation is to adapt the powerful prayers of the Apostle Paul as a model to pray for your children. Six prayers in Paul's New Testament Letters would be very appropriate to pray for your children regularly: Ephesians 1:16-19; 3:14-19; Philippians 1:9-11; Colossians 1:9-12; 2 Thessalonians 1:11-12; and Philemon 1:4-6. Utilize these prayers in sequential order from Monday through Saturday, week after week. For example, on Monday, use Ephesians 1:16-19 as a model prayer; on Tuesday Ephesians 3:14-19; on Wednesday

Philippians 1:9-11, and so forth. *Personalize each prayer for your children in your own words.*

Another recommendation is to pray that your children would grow in manifesting the Fruit of the Spirit found in Galatians 5:22-23: *"love, joy, peace, patience, kindness, goodness, faithfulness, gentleness, self-control."* There is a cluster of 9 godly virtues listed. Divide them into the days of the week Monday, love; Tuesday, joy and peace, and so on. As you pray, think of ways each of these godly virtues can be personalized in the lives of your children. Imagine the distinctive character of a person (prayerfully your child!) in whom the Spirit of God cultivates these wonderful qualities and virtues!

4. Partner with God's family, the church.

The church is the second most important spiritual influence in a child's life, right after the family. Gathering together with other believers is an integral part of the Christian life. Therefore, it should be a high priority. We are exhorted in Hebrews 10:24-25, *"And let us consider how to stir up one another to love and good works, not neglecting to meet together, as is the habit of some, but encouraging one another, and all the more as you see the Day drawing near."* Commit yourself and your family to a vibrant, Bible-believing church.

First Timothy 3:15 communicates the importance of the church by calling it *"the household of God, which is the church of the living God, a pillar and buttress of the truth."* The local church should be viewed as an extended family that loves and supports one another. Active involvement in a church that faithfully teaches the Word of God is a big help to families that desire to teach their children biblical truths and values on which to build their lives. Furthermore, people's lives being changed through saving faith in Jesus Christ, and the overall influence of godly men and women in the church who are living out their faith is a great encouragement for children to witness. This helps to confirm the conviction in your child's heart—"If so and so is passionate about their faith in Christ, then my parents must be right." Commitment to a Bible-teaching church can be a great support and encouragement to what they are learning at home.

As parents, we are responsible for setting the proper attitude toward the church because our attitude will affect our children's attitudes toward the church. Do your children see you rushing each Sunday morning to prepare for church, impatient and arguing? Is worship a duty or a joy? It is crucial that we do not convey that church is boring, a hassle on Sunday mornings, or show indifference to what is going on there. Realize that you have a significant amount of influence here, and your own attitude will speak loudly. Enthusiasm and willing participation will go a long way.

David and Karen Mains shared a simple but novel idea for experiencing more from church through a "game" they played each Sunday with their children.[6] There were three rules to the game. The *first rule* is to approach the church worship service with the expectation that God will speak to each member of the family. It may be through the sermon, Sunday school class, songs, or a casual conversation with someone before or after the worship service. The *second rule* is to discover how the Lord will speak through them to someone else. It may be by a comment shared in Sunday school, or an encouraging remark to someone going through a difficult time, or reaching out to someone new to the church. The *third rule* took place when they gathered again at home after church and sharing how the Lord spoke to them and through them. This simple "game" helped each family member become more fully engaged at church and experience it in a fresh way each week. It also helped them grow spiritually and strengthened them as a family. We encourage you to play this "game" with your children. It is a simple idea that can revolutionize your worship experience.

CHAPTER 8

The Means Parents are to Use in Instructing Children

Since it is so important to shape and guide our children's spiritual development, God has given them the capacity to receive and understand spiritual truths from an early age. When a child grabs hold of a life-changing truth from God's Word and internalizes it, it has the power to alter the course of his or her life. What follows are some realistic (and often neglected) ways parents can accomplish this.

1. **Make conversation about God and biblical truth common and natural in everyday experiences.**

Again, Deuteronomy 6:6-7 gives us a picture of this:

> *And these words that I command you today shall be on your heart. You shall teach them diligently to your children, and shall talk of them when you sit in your house, and when you walk by the way, and when you lie down, and when you rise.*

These verses emphasize that the Scriptures should be a regular topic of conversation in the day-to-day lives of our children: *"when you sit in your house, and when you walk by the way, and when you lie down, and when you rise."* God wants you to teach the Scriptures to your children in all kinds of places and in all types of circumstances, whenever and wherever life takes you. As the Bible Knowledge Commentary states, "The moral and biblical education of the children was accomplished best, not in a formal teaching period each day, but when the parents, out of concern for their own lives as well as their children's, made God and His Word the natural topic of conversation which might occur anywhere and anytime during the day."[7]

Many Christian parents compartmentalize the extent of the spiritual training of their children to formal family devotions or Sunday School at church. While formal instruction is important, times of informal instruction in ordinary conversations should not be overlooked. In fact, informal instruction can be more effective because it often speaks to what is going on in your child's life at that given moment. When the truth of God's Word is applied during life's experiences, it is usually grasped more readily.

Armand has been in pastoral ministry for several decades, and we are both certified biblical counselors. As a result, we have been involved in the lives of many people through the years, and we have been struck by the fact that many Christian families do not talk about the Lord and His Word in the home. Do not limit or compartmentalize your walk with the Lord to Sunday morning church or even family devotions. Talk freely about your relationship with Christ in the home. Casual and impromptu remarks are a good way to share what God is teaching you. Share an insight you have gleaned from God's Word. It will inadvertently have an impact on your children more than what you may think, and more than what they may let you know.

Make conversation about God and biblical truth common and natural in everyday experiences. Establish this as a normal pattern of family life. Children need to know that mom and dad are committed to Christ in everyday life. Prayerfully, the goal is that faith becomes a natural part of our children's daily lives, instead of just giving the impression that our faith is just what you do on Sundays.

Above the fireplace mantel in our home is a plaque that we treasure. It was given to us from our children and their spouses at Armand's retirement party from his long-held senior pastor position. The inscription on the plaque is a quotation from Psalm 78:4:

We will not hide them from their children,
but tell to the coming generation
the glorious deeds of the Lord, and his might,
and the wonders that he has done.
Psalm 78:4

We thank you, Dad and Mom, for the
spiritual heritage you have given us.

Christian parents have the privilege and solemn obligation to instill a spiritual heritage in their children. Making conversation about God and biblical truth a part of everyday life helps to instill that spiritual heritage. The next point expands on this.

2. Be alert to teachable moments in the lives of your children.

By this, we mean, be alert to ways of connecting biblical truth to life's events (without overdoing it, giving a lecture, or being too preachy). There are going to be times in the lives of your children when their hearts will be especially open to the truth of God's Word on various matters. Take advantage of these opportunities! For example,

- If another child gets into trouble because of bad behavior or an older person they know gets into trouble with the law, it can be a teachable moment for your child as they see an example of where sin leads. It is an opportunity to explain to your child why the Bible warns us of the terrible consequences of sin (see Proverbs 1:32-33; 5:21-23; 10:23; 13:20; 14:16; Romans 6:23; Galatians 6:7-8).

- If your child is engaged in sibling rivalry or conflict with a friend, it is a teachable moment. It is an opportunity to teach your child what the Bible says about confessing their wrongdoing, how to forgive others who have wronged them, and how to reconcile differences with others (see Proverbs 15:1; 20:3; 28:13; Matthew 5:23-24; Luke 17:3-4;John 13:34; Romans 12:18; Ephesians 4:1-3, 31-32; Colossians 3:13; 1 Thessalonians 5:15; James 5:16; 1 Peter 4:8).

- When your child faces a trial or a difficult circumstance and they become fearful and anxious, it is an opportunity to teach your child how to overcome worry and anxiety by trusting in a sovereign God; how He is in absolute control over all things, so they do not have to be fearful or anxious. God is sufficient to meet their need. If they put their trust in Him, He will give them the strength to get through any difficulty, and use it to deepen their faith and perfect their character (see Joshua 1:9; Isaiah 26:3; 41:10; Romans 8:18, 28; 2 Corinthians 4:16-18; Philippians 4:7; James 1:2-4, 12; 1 Peter 1:6-7).

- If someone they know is suffering through hard times, teach them to reach out to a friend in need with the love of Christ (see Matthew 5:14-16; 25:40; Luke 6:38; 10:30-37; Galatians 6:2; Philippians 2:4; Hebrews 13:16; 1 John 3:17).

- When your unredeemed child continues to struggle with sinful behavior and attitudes, this can be an opportunity to share with them their need for the Savior (Romans 3:23; 5:8; 6:23; 10:9-10, 13). Through a saving relationship with Jesus Christ, they can be freed from the power of sin and empowered by the Holy Spirit to overcome sinful habits, thoughts, and tendencies (Romans 6:1-14; 8:1-14; 2 Corinthians 5:17).

In other words, we are to teach our children how to apply the truths of Scripture to the things they face in life, helping them grow into mature, godly adults, *"complete and equipped for every good work"* (2 Timothy 3:14-17). These teachable moments make Scripture come alive for your child, and infuse the truth of God's Word into their hearts.

3. Pray with your children.

Many of the teachable moments in the lives of your children will give opportunities to pause and pray with them. Pray with them about the things they are facing, about the hard lessons of life that they are learning, about the issues they are facing at school, or a conflict they are having with a friend, etc. Praying with them over such things nurtures the relationship with your children because it lets them see that you are concerned about what concerns them. Furthermore, by praying with your children, you are inadvertently teaching them how to pray, and the need to rely upon God and His presence in their lives. That is a legacy worth leaving!

4. Discuss common challenges to the Christian faith.

- How do you know God exists?
- How do you know the Bible is true?
- If God is good, why does He allow evil and suffering?
- Hasn't science disproved the Christian faith?

Any thinking child is going to question the validity of the Christian faith. They may even have moments of doubt. These questions that cause doubts are part of growing in the faith. Our children need to personalize their faith in Christ, not merely live on the borrowed faith of their parents. Therefore, parents should not panic and overreact if a child is questioning the Christian faith. Resist the temptation to lecture. Calmly listen to their question or objection concerning the faith. Then gently explain what you believe and why. Do not offer shallow answers or clichés, such as, "You just have to believe." In fact, we recommend from time to time that you bring up a common challenge to the Christian faith, and discuss it with your children. Doing so will not only encourage their faith but also prepare them for a time when it may come up in other settings.

The Bible urges us to *"always be prepared to make a defense to anyone who asks you for a reason for the hope that is in you; yet do it with gentleness and respect"* (1 Peter 3:15). These are great opportunities for conversations concerning evidence for the Christian faith. In fact, it will sharpen your own understanding of the faith. If you do not know the answer to a question, do some research or talk to your pastor.[8] If your child is a teenager, read a biblically solid book with them on Christian apologetics to explore their questions of faith together. This can serve as a time of relationship building with your child as you shepherd them through their questions. These conversations concerning common objections to the faith with your children are opportunities to deepen their trust and confidence in God and His Word.

5. Point your children to the living hope we have in Christ.

> *Blessed be the God and Father of our Lord Jesus Christ! According to his great mercy, he has caused us to be born again to a living hope through the resurrection of Jesus Christ from the dead, to an inheritance that is imperishable, undefiled, and unfading, kept in heaven for you, who by God's power are being guarded through faith for a salvation ready to be revealed in the last time. In this you rejoice, though now for a little while, if necessary, you have been grieved by various trials, so that the tested genuineness of your faith—more precious than gold that perishes though it is tested by fire—may be found to result in praise and glory and honor at the revelation of Jesus Christ.*
>
> *1 Peter 1:3-7*

Children need the hope for their personal lives that only Jesus Christ can give. Every family, spouse, friendship, or group that they identify with will eventually fall short and disappoint in some way. What our children ultimately need is an intimate relationship with the Only One who will not fall short and disappoint.

Nothing should be closer to your heart as a Christian parent than helping your children come to saving faith in Christ. As mentioned, you should be regularly praying for your children's salvation. And, as you do this, you should explain as much of the Gospel to them as they can understand for their age. They need to know that they are sinners in need of the Savior (Romans 3:23). As they begin to understand the sinful propensity of their hearts, it will be the truth of the Gospel that will give them hope. Help your child know that a relationship with Jesus Christ begins through saving faith. Faith in the atoning work of Christ on the cross and His victorious resurrection from the grave gives them the assurance that their sins have been forgiven, and the blessed hope of eternal life. Use day-to-day life as opportunities to share the Gospel with your children. For example, as you faithfully discipline them for misbehavior, use this as an opportunity to point them to their need for a Savior. Another occasion could be when one of your children is walking through a time of trial and suffering. It could be used as an opportunity to tell them of the great love and compassion that Jesus displayed for them when He suffered and died in their place.

Additionally, children need the hope that will sustain them in their day-to-day life; *the hope that God will be with them throughout all the ups and downs they will experience* (Hebrews 13:5), *and the hope that God is at work making them more and more like Christ* (2 Corinthians 3:18). This is the hope that sustained our daughter, Anna. At the age of nineteen, while on an overseas mission trip, she became seriously ill. She was diagnosed with Type 1 diabetes. Alone in the hospital, in a foreign land, it was the hope of Christ that sustained her during this challenging and life-altering trial.

Assure your children that God is at work in them. He can turn their liabilities into assets and their emptiness into fullness; that a better life follows this one! You, as a parent, can assure them: "You're going to grow in Christ more and more. We look forward to seeing the person in the Lord you are going to be." Proverbs 4:18 assures us, *"But the path of the righteous is like the light of dawn, which shines brighter and brighter until full day."* Children need to know that God is with them and at work, making them more and more like Christ. Nurture this wonderful hope in your children!

CHAPTER 9

Nine Essential Life Lessons to Teach Your Children

One of the most helpful books in the Bible for instilling biblical truths and values into the lives of our children is the Book of Proverbs. One of its major themes has to do with parental responsibility. It is a resource and guidebook for parents. The keyword in Proverbs is *wisdom — skill in right living.* It is concerned with the development of godly attributes. The purpose of Proverbs is stated in 1:1-6. In brief, it is to give godly wisdom and character to youth so that they will find true blessedness in life and avoid the snares and pitfalls of sin.

What we see in these opening words of Proverbs is a father and a mother instructing a child: *"Hear, my son, your father's instruction, and forsake not your mother's teaching ..."* (1:8). Godly parental instruction is a repeated theme in Proverbs (e.g., see 2:1; 3:1; 4:1; 5:1; 6:1; 7:1). It shows the responsibility of parents to instruct their children in the way of the Lord. Parents should not rob their children of this valuable instruction.

Notice how valuable godly instruction is: *"Take my instruction instead of silver, and knowledge rather than choice gold, for wisdom is better than jewels, and all that you may desire cannot compare with her"* (8:10-11; cf. 2:1-9, 12, 16, 20). The most valuable asset a young person can attain is the wisdom to order his or her life according to God's ways. God says that godly instruction is of much greater value than anything else a child can receive from the home.

What follows are a summary and Scripture references of vital areas of instruction children should be taught by parents during the tender growing-up-years. Of course, they are not the only things that children should be taught. But each of these is chosen because they are repeated again and again in Proverbs. Repeated instruction on one lesson reveals the importance of it.

1. **To instill reverence and devotion to God** (1:7; 3:7-8; 9:10; 10:27; 14:26-27; 15:33; 16:6b; 19:23; 31:30).

Fourteen times in Proverbs, we see that phrase, *"The fear of the Lord."* This is not referring to a cringing fear, but having trust and holy reverence for God that flows from recognizing His divine sovereignty over all things. It is living with a sense of responsibility and accountability before our Creator and Redeemer. Proverbs 9:10 tells us, *"The fear of the Lord is the beginning of wisdom."* A healthy fear of the Lord is where we begin our journey of wise living. Proverbs 14:26 assures us that when we understand the greatness of God, we will have strong confidence, and our children will have a place of refuge. Proverbs 16:6b says that a healthy fear of God keeps us from presumptuous sin because one day, we must all face Him.

From a very young age, children must be taught reverence for the holy God of Scripture. Instill in them a vision of God in all His power and majesty in words they can understand. Let your children sense the reverence, honor, and humility you have when you speak to and about God. A wise parent and child make decisions every day to walk and live with deep reverence and devotion to the Lord.

2. **To revere and obey the Word of God** (2:1-6; 3:1-2; 4:1-6, 20-22; 7:1-3; 13:13; 16:20; 19:16; 28:9; 30:5-6).

"Whoever despises the word brings destruction on himself, but he who reveres the commandment will be rewarded" (Proverbs 13:13). God blesses those who honor and obey His Word. Teach your children to revere and obey the Word of God, for it is the pathway of wisdom, life, and fruitfulness. Show them how much you value it by reading it regularly and sharing what God is teaching you. Let them see that your love for God's Word is real and that it helps you in your marriage, in resolving conflicts, and the choices that you make. Let them see how God's Word guides you as you make decisions, receive comfort, and face challenges. Let them know that the Word can do the same for them.

Kathy has a habit of putting Bible verses on post-it notes on the kitchen windowsill and her desk that she wants to memorize and meditate on for personal growth. As our children noticed the verses, they realized that God was working through His Word in her life. Our married daughter, Anna, now does the same at her desk.

3. **To impart the attributes of wisdom** (1:2-4; 2:1-12, 16; 3:21-24; 4:1-2, 5-9; 5:1-2; 8:5, 12; 9:4-6; 11:1, 22; 14:15-16; 27:12; 31:8-9).

The opening words of Proverbs set forth the purpose for which it was written: *"To know wisdom and instruction, to understand words of insight, to receive instruction in wise dealing, in righteousness, justice, and equity; to give prudence to the simple, knowledge and discretion to the youth"* (1:2-4).These are attributes children need to develop to live wisely, morally, and ethically in this world. As a child grows and develops these attributes of wisdom, they will be successful at living life, at facing the problems of life, and at making good choices in life. They will have the ability to discern truth from error, to perceive what is right or wrong, helpful or harmful, and how to make good, sound judgments, etc.

Wise parents will make good use of the Book of Proverbs. Focus on a pertinent verse during family devotions. It is interesting to note that there are 31 chapters in the book of Proverbs. When your children begin to enter into the teen years, encourage them to read a chapter a day from the Book of Proverbs. Read the chapter number that corresponds to the day of the month. Discuss any verse(s) that they found to be particularly significant. Doing so will impart nuggets of wisdom in their precious minds, which will shape their thinking, behavior, and lives.

4. **To honor and obey their parents** (1:8; 4:1-4; 6:20-23; 20:20; 23:22-25; 30:11, 17; 31:26-28).

This is one of the most obvious (yet neglected) responsibilities of parents. Honor and obey are not qualities that children will automatically develop. This is why Proverbs is filled with statements like, *"Hear, my son, your father's instruction, and forsake not your mother's teaching"* (reinforcing the fifth commandment to *"Honor your father and your mother").* It is the responsibility of parents to train their children to honor and obey them. This will involve not only verbal instruction but also correction and discipline tempered by love (cf. 3:11-12; 13:24). Failure to do so will result in the child following the way of foolishness and iniquity, which ends in destruction and death (14:12; 20:20), and sorrow for the parents (17:21, 25). Honoring and obeying parents follows the way of wisdom and righteousness, which leads to reward and life (6:20-23; 9:6; 12:28). Additionally, when children learn to honor and obey, they will bring happiness to their parents (23:24-25), learn to honor and obey human authority, and, more importantly, this is how they learn to honor and obey God.

5. **To consider their words carefully** (4:24; 10:11, 19-21, 31-32; 12:17-19, 22; 13:3; 15:1-2, 4,23, 28; 16:23-24; 17:27-28; 18:2, 6-8, 21; 21:23; 25:11; 29:11, 20).

"To make an apt answer is a joy to a man, and a word in season, how good it is" (15:23). *"The heart of the righteous ponders how to answer"* (15:28). There are approximately 150 references in Proverbs about the words we speak and how we speak them. It stands to reason that any topic mentioned that often is of vital importance. As Proverbs 18:21 states, *"Death and life are in the power of the tongue."* Our words have the power to bless or curse, build up or destroy, speak the truth or deceive, comfort or provoke! As parents, we set the example for our children by the way we communicate within the home. By God's grace, we should always be seeking to grow in this area of our lives.

Here are a few helpful reminders from Proverbs concerning godly and ungodly communication:

- *There is one whose rash words are like sword thrusts, but the tongue of the wise brings healing (12:18).*

- *Lying lips are an abomination to the Lord, but those who act faithfully are his delight (12:22).*
- *A soft answer turns away wrath, but a harsh word stirs up anger (15:1).*
- *Gracious words are like a honeycomb, sweetness to the soul and health to the body (16:24).*
- *A fool's lips walk into a fight, and his mouth invites a beating (18:6).*
- *A fool's mouth is his ruin, and his lips are a snare to his soul (18:7).*
- *Whoever keeps his mouth and his tongue keeps himself out of trouble (21:23).*

There are so many applicable lessons in Proverbs concerning the use of our words. A spiritually profitable exercise to do with your children is to look up the Scripture references listed after the title in number 5 above. Write in your own words what each verse teaches about godly or ungodly communication, and the positive or negative impact it would have on your life and others. Prayerfully, such an exercise would significantly affect both you and your child to consider your words carefully.

Furthermore, the THINK acronym would be helpful to teach to your children and can be posted on a wall:

Before you speak.... THINK!

T – is it true?
H – is it helpful?
I – is it inspiring?
N – is it necessary?
K – is it kind?

If your children grow into adulthood and have learned this vital lesson—to consider their words carefully—they will not suffer many of the negative consequences of the uncontrolled tongue, and minimize many relational conflicts. Positively, they will be viewed as a person of good repute, will have success in life, and find favor in the sight of man and God (cf. 3:1-4).

6. **To have a good work ethic** (6:6-11; 10:4-5; 12:11, 24; 13:4; 18:9; 20:4, 13; 21:5; 22:29; 24:30-34; 26:13-16).

"The soul of the sluggard craves and gets nothing, while the soul of the diligent is richly supplied" (Proverbs 13:4). A subject matter that Proverbs returns to over and over again is the contrast between laziness and diligence. The father in Proverbs taught his son to have a good work ethic, so when he enters into adulthood, he will provide for the needs of his household and avoid the hard consequences of laziness. Unfortunately, this is lacking in our day and age. Parents must not permit their children to develop habits of idleness and slothfulness.

Children raised to appreciate the value of work tend to be more responsible in other areas of life. Giving children household chores is a good way of teaching your children how to be diligent. They can begin to learn a good work ethic at an early age. For example, a 3-year-old can put their toys in the toy box at the end of the day. A 6 or 7-year-old should be able to make their bed. Older children can vacuum, empty the dishwasher, or mow the lawn. And, of course, praise and appreciation for the completed task can go a long way in motivating a child to pursue a good work ethic.

7. **To manage money wisely** (3:9-10; 6:1-5; 10:2; 11:24-26, 28; 13:11; 15: 6, 16, 27; 19:17; 21:5-6, 20; 22:1, 7, 9; 23:4-5; 28:19-20, 25, 27).

Money plays a prominent role in life. That is why Proverbs speaks so often about how we are to manage it. If we manage it wisely, it can be a means of blessing. However, if we are careless, money can become the source of much anxiety and heartache. Many adults get into financial trouble because they did not learn this valuable lesson in childhood.

When children earn some money or are given a weekly allowance, it is an opportunity to teach them three basic principles of money management. *First* and foremost is the principle of tithing. Proverbs 3:9-10 teaches that those who honor God with their money will be blessed in return. We honor God by giving a portion of our income to His work. *Second,* Proverbs 21:5 and 27:23-24 teaches the principle of budgeting—keeping track of the finances God has entrusted to us. In other words, plan your spending carefully, and you will have plenty, but if you spend too hastily, you will never have enough. The *third* is the principle of saving. Proverbs 6:6-8 illustrates the wisdom in providing for future needs — to have a buffer when the unexpected happens.

By giving your children a good head-start in wise money management, prayerfully, they will grow up with a sense of responsibility in money matters and avoid many of the pitfalls and consequences of mismanagement.

8. **To choose companions wisely** (1:10-18; 2:10-15, 20; 4:14-15; 13:20; 14:7; 20:19; 22:5, 24-25; 23:20-21; 24:1-2).

Time and again, the father in Proverbs warns his son about the harmful influence of evil companions. Right up front, he says, *"My son, if sinners entice you, do not consent"* (1:10). Negative peer pressure can have a strong influence on a child's attitude and behavior. Proverbs 13:20 clearly teaches, *"Whoever walks with the wise becomes wise, but the companion of fools will suffer harm"* (cf. 1 Corinthians 15:33). Therefore, equip your children with social wisdom so they will develop discretion in choosing friends(2:10-15). Children need to learn to discern who will enhance, rather than inhibit, their personal spiritual growth and relationship with God.

There are several ways parents can be proactive in this:

- Be hospitable to your children's friends. Become acquainted with them so you will have a reasonable understanding of what is going on when they play together.

- Encourage your children to influence their non-Christian friends, rather than be influenced by them.

- Be realistic. Since no one is perfect, we do not want our children to have expectations of a friend that is so high that no one can live up to it.

- Help your children prepare in advance for what they should do if they are visiting a friend's house and are being exposed to something inappropriate, such as a movie, Internet website, vulgar language, type of play or activity, or improper behavior on the part of the adults or an older child in the home. Teach them to text, call home, or leave, if possible.

9. **To live a sexually moral life** (2:16-19; 5:1-23; 6:23-35; 7:1-27; 9:13-18; 11:22; 12:4; 22:14; 23:27-28; 29:3; 30:20).

The father in Proverbs speaks very candidly to his son about the dangers of sexual immorality: *"Can a man carry fire next to his chest and his clothes not be burned?"* (6:27). *"He who commits adultery lacks sense; he who does it destroys himself"* (6:32). Parental warnings against sexual immorality are one of the most dominant themes in the first 9 chapters of Proverbs. Wise parents realize that puberty is a time when sexual desires are heightened. Since we live in a sex-obsessed culture, it is tempting for our children to become sexually promiscuous by simply following the crowd. Therefore, the danger of sexual sin and the beauty of sexual purity is a truth all parents need to teach their children.

There are many exhortations in Proverbs that you can use to instruct your children toward sexual purity. What follows are some key bullet points from major passages. Although they are exhortations of a father to his son, the same principles apply to mothers and daughters.

Chapter 2:16-19:

- Verse 17 implies that sexual sin is contrary to God's design for human relationships, and a violation of the seventh commandment given by God in Exodus 20:14.
- God knows that sexual sin has power to hurt us. It has devastated countless lives and destroyed many marriages and families (18-19). He wants to protect us from hindering our fellowship with Him and from hurting ourselves and others.

Chapter 5:1-23:

- Wisdom, understanding, discretion, and knowledge will keep us from being seduced by the façade of flattery and smooth words (1-2).
- A wise person will stay far away from tempting environments and the sexually immoral (7-8; cf. 4:25-27). It can lead to a sexually transmitted disease, or divine chastisement and even lead to death (3-6, 11-12), and a life full of guilt and woes for not obeying the ways and wisdom of God (9-14, 20-23).
- God knows all about our sin in heart and actions (21).
- Sexual delight and pleasure in marriage are good and encouraged. God's plan is for a husband and wife to find sexual satisfaction and enjoyment from each other (15-19).

Chapter 6:20-35:

- Do not entertain lustful desires in your heart for another person (23-25; cf. Matthew 5:27-28).

- See past the temptation of momentary illicit pleasure to the long-term consequences and repercussions it will result in.
- Spiritual ruin, loss of purity, social disgrace, financial loss, and jealous revenge from another person are potential consequences of sexual sin (26-35).
- Proverbs 6:27-28 would be pertinent verses to memorize for guarding the heart against sexual immorality.

Chapter 7:1-27:

- God's Word is meant to protect us from the hurt and harm caused by sexual sin (1-5).
- Exhortations include keeping off the path that one knows will lead to sexual temptation (4-9, 24-25) because it leads to enslavement, ruin, and ultimately God's judgment if not repented of (22-23, 26-27).
- Again, beware of flattery, smooth talk, and seductive speech designed to draw us into sexual sin (21).

Realize that your children will get unbiblical teaching about sex from a variety of sources, such as conversations with friends, TV, music, the Internet, etc. Therefore, you must be sure that your children are getting a Christ-centered understanding of sexuality. Some relevant questions to discuss with your children at the appropriate age would include:

- What does God say is right and wrong behavior toward members of the opposite sex?

- Why is pre-marital sex and adultery wrong? What harm do they do?

- Why is sexual purity before marriage right?
  What good does it do?

- Why is faithfulness in marriage right?
  What good does it do?

These are some significant lessons from Proverbs that children should be taught. It should be obvious that if you intentionally pass on these vital truths to your children during their formative years, it would save them from many woes of life. It would have a positive effect on their character and the godly heritage they carry into adulthood.

The father of the righteous will greatly rejoice;
He who fathers a wise son will be glad in him.
Let your father and mother be glad; let her who bore you rejoice.
Proverbs 23:24-25

Conclusion

We hope and pray that these three essential elements modeled by our heavenly Father have given you a passion and practical direction for being intentional in cultivating a good family heritage for your children. Investing in our children is worth our very best efforts. There is no greater earthly blessing than raising children in a way that honors and glorifies God and seeing them grow up to honor and glorify God with their own lives and passing on that same legacy to their children.

At the end of this booklet is a list of recommended resources for further study that will help you in this great task. May God richly bless your efforts and your family!

Feedback from Parents who Read the Book

This book was a timely blessing in my life! It hit some target areas that I have wanted to grow in as a mother. It offers real, practical ways to apply the biblical truths that are taught. I definitely think it will both inspire and challenge the moms and dads that read it.

Esther Geletka and her husband are raising five children.

The booklet was wonderful and very encouraging! It personally ministered to us in more ways that can be mentioned in this blurb. It's easy to read, yet insightful, challenging, motivating, and gives lots of practical advice. It is a wonderful resource for parents desiring to leave a great heritage to their children.

Mike and Anna DiSanto, Parents of two young adopted children.

I really enjoyed this book. It is very balanced in giving a biblical description of a godly family, but also filled with very practical ideas of how to put some healthy patterns into practice. I can see this being a helpful tool to put into the hands of many young families who are seeking to be intentional in cultivating a heritage with the time that they have with their children.

Luke Rosenberger, Lead Pastor, Cornerstone Bible Church, Middlefield, Ohio. Luke and his wife are in the midst of raising five children.

Recommended Resources for Further Study

1. Resources for Cultivating a Spirit of Belonging and Connectedness in Family Relationships

John Crotts, *Mighty Men: The Starter's Guide to Leading Your Family* (Sand Springs, Ok: Grace & Truth Books, 2004).

Emily Jensen and Laura Wifler, *Risen Motherhood: Gospel Hope for Everyday Moments* (Eugene, OR: Harvest House Publishers, 2019).

Martha Peace, *The Excellent Wife* (Bemidji, MN: Focus Publishing, Revised Edition, 1999).

Stuart Scott, *The Exemplary Husband* (Bemidji, MN: Focus Publishing, Revised Edition, 2002).

Paul and Karen Tautges, *Help! My Toddler Rules the House* (Wapwallopen, PA: 2010).

Paul Tautges, *Raising Kids in a You Can Do It World* (Leyland, England: 10 Publishing, 2018).

Armand Tiffe, *Transformed into His Likeness: A Handbook for Putting Off Sin and Putting On Righteousness* (Bemidji, MN: Focus Publishing, Revised Edition 2018).

Paul David Tripp, *Parenting: Gospel Principles That Can Radically Change Your Family* (Wheaton, IL: Crossway, 2016).

Tedd Tripp, *Shepherding a Child's Heart* (Wapwallopen, PA: Shepherd Press, 1995)

2. Resources for Sowing Seeds that Reap Cherished Memories

Gloria Gaither and Shirley Dobson, *Creating Family Traditions: Making Memories in Festive Seasons* (Sisters, OR: Multnomah, 2004).

Noel Piper, *Treasuring God in Our Traditions* (Wheaton, Il: Crossway, 2003).

Jessica Smartt, *Memory-Making Mom: Building Traditions that Breathe Life into Your Home* (Thomas Nelson, 2019).

3. Resources for Instilling Biblical Truth and Values into the Lives of Your Children

Natasha Crain, *Keeping Your Kids on God's Side: 40 Conversations to Help Them Build a Lasting Faith,* (Harvest House Publishers, 2016).

Kara Durbin, *Parenting with Scripture: A Topical Guide for Teachable Moments* (Chicago, IL, Moody, 2012).

Got Questions is a helpful online resource that answers many questions about the Christian faith: www.gotquestions.org

David Helm, *Small Devotionals, Big Beliefs: Introducing Your Family to Big Truths* (Phillipsburg, NJ: P & R Publishing, 2016).

Jack Klumpenhower, *Show Them Jesus: Teaching the Gospel to Kids* (Greensboro, NC: New Growth Press, 2014).

Marty Machowski, *Leading Your Child to Christ: Biblical*

Direction for Sharing the Gospel (Greensboro, NC: New Growth Press, 2012).

Jim Newheiser, *Help! I Need a Church* (Wapwallopen, PA: Shepherd Press, 2016).

Lou Priolo, *Teach Them Diligently: How to Use Scriptures in Child Training* (Sand Springs, OK: Grace and Truth Books, 2000).

John Stonestreet and Brett Kunkle, *A Student's Guide to Culture* (David C Cook, 2020).

John Younts, *Everyday Talk: Talking Freely and Naturally about God with Your Children* (Wapwallopen, PA: Shepherd Press, 2004).